AS THE MORNING STAR

"Quasi stella matutina in medio nebulæ, et quasi luna plena, in diebus suis lucet; et quasi sol refulgens, sic ille effulsit in templo Dei."

"He shone in his days As THE MORNING STAR in the midst of a cloud, and as the moon at the full. And as the sun when it shineth, so did he shine in the temple of God".

—SIRACH 50:6-7

AS THE MORNING STAR

❀❀❀❀❀❀❀❀❀

THE LIFE OF ST. DOMINIC

Rev. Jerome Wilms, O.P.

Translated from the German
by a Dominican Sister of the Perpetual Rosary
Milwaukee, Wisconsin

MEDIATRIX PRESS
MMXIV

ISBN: 978-1-953746-07-8

Mediatrix Press
607 E. 6th Ave.
Post Falls, ID 83854

TABLE OF CONTENTS

FOREWORD i

THE AUTHOR v

I SEEDTIME OF LIFE

      CALAROCA 1

      GUMIEL DE IZAN 6

      PALENCIA 8

      O S M A 12

II IN THE RETINUE OF BLESSED DIEGO

      THE AQUITANIAN JOURNEY 17

      CITEAUX 20

      MONTPELLIER 21

      MONTREAL 25

      PROUILLE 28

III PEACEFUL LABORS IN WARTIME

CARCASSONNE. 33

MURET 38

TOULOUSE. 42

IV THE FOUNDATION OF THE ORDER OF
PREACHERS

THE DECREE OF THE LATERAN
COUNCIL 47

THE RULE OF ST. AUGUSTINE. 50

THE CONSTITUTIONS OF THE ORDER
OF PREACHERS. 53

PAPAL APPROBATION 56

V THE DISPERSION OF THE BRETHREN

PROUILLE AS MONASTERY OF THE
SECOND ORDER
. . . . 59

MADRID AND SEGOVIA 64

PARIS. 69

BOLOGNA 72

ROME. 76

VI THE EXPANSION OF THE ORDER

    THE INNER DEVELOPMENT 81

    EXTERIOR PROPAGATION.......... 86

VII LIFE'S CLOSE

    ILLNESS AND DEATH 91

    GLORIFICATION................... 94

VIII THE PERSONALITY

    THE MAN........................ 99

    THE ASCETIC 101

    THE MYSTIC 104

    THE APOSTLE................... 107

    THE SAINT..................... 109

FOREWORD

FOR many years, owing to a lack of the necessary source materials, it was practically impossible to write a life of St. Dominic which would meet with the requirements of modern hagiography. The requisite documents and publications were not available. The establishment of the Dominican Historical Institute in Rome after World War I was, therefore, greeted with a Te Deum by many students. In the *Monumenta Fratrum Praedicatorum Historica*, Tom. XV, are contained Father Hyacinth Laurent's History of Our Holy Father St. Dominic (Paris: J. Vrin, 1933); Dr. H. C. Scheeben's Beginnings of the Order of Preachers from the original of Blessed Jordan of Saxony; Father Angelus Walz's Acts of Canonization; Father Hyacinth Laurent's History of St. Dominic From the Original of Peter Ferandi; Dr. H. C. Scheeben's History of St. Dominic from the original of Constantine of Orvieto; Father Angelus Walz's History of St. Dominic from the original of Humbert the Roman (Rome, 1935, Convent of Santa Sabina).

These sources Dr. Scheeben uses in his book, St. Dominic (Freiburg: Herder, 1927), to give a picture of the century in which St. Dominic lived and worked. The present writing does not aim to emulate Lacordaire's beauty of style and expression. Neither does it propose to supplant Dr. Scheeben's work, described as follows in its Preface

i

by Father Walz. "The Dominican history has been set forth by an author who so completely submerged himself in the environment, stature, and spirit of the Saint from Calaroga as to succeed in giving an attractive, true-to-life picture of the Saint's personality and character, which radiated light, magnetic power, and sacred, priestly zeal for souls." However, the fountain bubbles continuously, and so accounts and depositions permit sundry interpretations. Consequently, the present book sometimes digresses from Dr. Scheeben's explanations, something that very probably will be true with every future life of St. Dominic. Everyone abounds in his own sentiments.

That after seven hundred years his life is still the subject of historians' endeavors is a clear proof of the deep significance of St. Dominic's personality for his Order, for the clergy, and the entire Church. He lived in the late Middle Ages, when the Chair of Peter was occupied by popes like Innocent III, whose prudence and firmness were active factors in shaping Europe's history. Christianity had not yet been split up by the Protestant Revolt. The spirit of faith still had at least a little influence in political matters, and enthusiasm for the reclaiming of the Holy Land swayed men's hearts. However, there were also ominous signs that a religious retrogression had begun. The Balkan countries and almost all of Spain were under the dominion of the Moors. Heretics were stirring up trouble in different localities. Monastic discipline had become relaxed. Spiritual ministrations were being neglected, because the clergy were either entangled in worldly matters or had succumbed to the easy life made available to them by their rich revenues. The ancient landed property of the Church excited the greed of the pious donors' less devout offspring. Revolutionary ideas, hostile to the faith, were being propagated and put into practice, and well-disposed individuals were too ignorant of religious principles to steer themselves out of this dangerous current.

By means of General Councils and Diocesan Synods, the Church had issued strict moral decrees for priests and religious concerning their pastoral duties and especially the preaching of the Gospel; but the end was not attained by merely issuing these decrees. Dominic was a man of action. He realized the need of the age and chose as his particular lifework the preaching of the Gospel. He established an Order, dedicated entirely to the salvation of souls by means of teaching and preaching the Word of God. Such an establishment was a grim necessity at that period — as it will be until the crack of doom. With this foundation Dominic introduced an entirely new element into the history of religious orders. He retained the community life and solemn choral prayer of the Augustinian canons and adopted many austerities from the old monastic orders, but added to all this the stipulation that the particular task of his followers would be the salvation of their fellow men. For that purpose he obliged his disciples to devote themselves, rain or shine, to study and preaching. His ideal, and that of his Order, is the Saviour spending His nights in prayer on the mountain, and traversing the countryside by day, announcing the tidings of salvation to all mankind.

Dominic became the patriarch of apostolic orders. To all with whom he came in contact, to his brethren and to outsiders, he was in truth an openhanded and large-hearted Father, wonderfully indulgent, but at the same time not yielding an inch in those things which mature deliberation had convinced him were necessary, and ready to attempt squaring a circle in order to carry out a worthy undertaking. Such a man has much to tell our own generation, perhaps everything needed for a genuine renewal.

THE AUTHOR

THE author of the present book, Rev. Jerome Wilms, O.P., was born July 6, 1878, in Grünhoven, near Rheydt, Germany, the son of William Wilms. After being graduated from the grade school in his native town he went to the Gymnasium (high school) in Rheindahlen, Venlo, Paderborn. He entered the Order of Friars Preachers and received the habit on September 9, 1897, made his simple profession a year later, and pronounced his solemn vows in Düsseldorf on September 24, 1901. He was ordained a priest in the chapel of the Diocesan Seminary of Cologne on August 14, 1904.

Father Jerome was appointed Lector in Dusseldorf in 1906 and served as headmaster of the Albertinum in Venlo from 1909 to 1915. From 1915 to 1930 he was Master of Novices, except for one year, 1919 to 1920, when he acted as Provincial of the German Dominican Province, called Teutonia. Father Jerome has written many books and pamphlets, and a few years ago the rarely bestowed degree of the Dominican Order, that of Master of Sacred Theology, was conferred upon him.

I
SEEDTIME OF LIFE

CALAROCA

"IN STUDYING the life of a man it is much to the historian's purpose to seek out the childhood of his subject, the skies which his youthful eyes first beheld, the woods and rivers which fascinated his imagination. The motive of this search is not curiosity, but the conviction that these factors hold the answers to many of life's enigmas." So writes Alfred Kuhn in his book, Old Spain.

Most of Dominic's manhood was spent on the roads of various European countries. When he was asked whence he came, his reply was always, "Spain is my fatherland." He was therefore a native of the Iberian Peninsula in southwestern Europe. This peninsula's connection with the continent is outlined by the peaks of the eastern Pyrenees, which extend from Cape Creux on the Mediterranean Sea to the Garonne River in France. Passage over this huge stone wall between Spain and France is extremely difficult. In the Middle Ages the paths that crossed the formidably gaping crags of this perpetually ice-covered Southern Chain were impassable except to pack mules and men on foot. The water route from Pampelone in northern Spain through Bayonne in southern France via the Bay of Biscay was more frequently used than the footpaths. It was in this way that the

1

Celts came to Spain from France toward the year 1000 B.C., and in the fifth century A.D. the Visigoths under Theodoric and Euric poured into Spain from this entrance. They had been preceded by the Vandals, the Suevians, and the Alani. The same stimuli had spurred on these various peoples: they came to rob, plunder, conquer, and finally to settle down. When the Moors invaded the country from the south at the beginning of the eighth century, a large number of Spanish Catholics sought refuge beyond the Pyrenees in France.

In the latter half of the eighth century Charlemagne was the most powerful monarch in western Europe; therefore, foreign rulers needing military aid often asked his assistance. This was the reason why Charlemagne several times penetrated into Spain with the object of breaking Moorish power and mastering part of the country. On one of these expeditions against the fortress city of Saragossa, with whose Moorish leader he had a pact, the Emperor suffered a setback. When his army came in sight of Saragossa, the city, instead of receiving him as agreed, closed its gates and prepared for defense. Thereupon Charlemagne decided to return to France. He withdrew through the Pass of Roncesvalles in the Pyrenees of Navarre, and there the Navarrese natives, or possibly Moorish troops, attacked the rearguard of the Franks and almost annihilated them. This was in 778. The incident gave rise to the Legend of Roland, a Frankish military leader who, in fact, was slain in the combat. During the reign of

Charlemagne's son, Louis the Pious (778-840), almost all the important cities of Spain were recaptured from the Moors and organized into a Frankish province called the Spanish March. France and all Europe received in return for their help countless benefits from Spain; not the least of these blessings was bestowed by means of the strange traveling preacher Dominic, who so frequently responded to the query, "Where are you from?" with the simple reply, "Spain is my fatherland."

"My parental home is in Castile," was the Spanish preacher's answer to further questioning about his birthplace. Alexander of Humboldt, an eighteenth-century German scientist and traveler, described Spain as a "granite plateau with a range of mountains dividing it in the center." This is particularly true of Castile, a tableland in the northern half of the Iberian Peninsula, completely surrounded by mountains. It is bounded on the north by the Cantabrian Range, on the west by the Estremadura, on the south by the Sierra Morena, and on the east by the Iberian Mountains. The Sierra de Gredos and the Guadarrama divide the region into New and Old Castile. The territory is covered with ice and snow during the winter months and parched by the sun in summer. Much of Old Castile is desert land. The rocky surface shows the result of the primeval glacial sheets which covered the land; indeed, one gets the impression that this region is the source of all Europe's stone supply. On most of this barren land only colorless steppe grass grows and supplies a meager existence to the frugal Merino sheep; but there are also oasis-like sections of great fertility, where almond and orange trees flourish and where grain and vegetables can be raised in abundance. These bountiful regions lured primitive barbarian tribes. This fertility, which had also attracted the Celts from France, was the reason why the Romans later guarded this colony with such particular diligence that Rome was named the "Imperial Nursing Mother." During the Roman occupation in the second century a system of irrigation was established, intended to extend the borders of these oasis-like districts. Although the Romans brought with them their culture and language, they did not intermarry with the country people, and so did not give the territory a permanent ruling class. The Visigoths, on the contrary, after renouncing Arianism and embracing the Catholic faith as preached to the primitive inhabitants by the Apostles James and Paul, mingled freely with the people and left a lasting influence on the country's language, culture, and political destiny.

However, Castile did not receive its name from either the Romans or the Visigoths, neither from the soil's fertility nor the summer's violent heat and the winter's biting cold, but from the fortified castles, castilla, which were erected throughout the country during the Moorish Wars to safeguard the territory against this archenemy of Christendom. After their defeat at Toulouse in 1212 the power of the Moors rapidly declined and the Christian forces extended their boundaries as far as the Kingdom of Granada. With the restoration of peace these fortress-like castles were no longer used for their original purpose, but the locality's name, Castile, would often remind parents to relate to their children their forefathers' brave deeds in defense of the faith.

Dominic's ancestors were among these combatants; as a matter of fact, his nearest relatives fought in the decisive battle of Toulouse and gave proof of their living faith and stouthearted chivalry. When questioned as to the city of his birth, Dominic would answer, "I was born in Calaroga." Calaroga, also called Caleruego, is situated on the road leading from Calatayud to Valladolid. It belongs to the diocese of Osma, only thirty miles distant. Today it has no more importance than a thousand other Spanish towns whose names are seldom heard in the United States. But that Calaroga was of considerable importance in the epoch which witnessed the country's deliverance from the Moors is testified even at the present day by the massive tower which the traveler can see several hours before he reaches the town. This tower is the last vestige of the castle where armed watch was maintained during the conflict. In 1266 King Alphonsus the Wise had the castle transformed into a monastery. Entirely separated from the world, cloistered Dominicans have ever since then hallowed those ancient precincts by their holy lives. Like other Blessed Cecilias, they keep alive the memory of St. Dominic, whose birth within this castle is its title to immortality, and with untiring enthusiasm they relate through the grille the particulars of their Blessed Father's life and death, prayer and preaching, to all who care to listen. According to the testimony of Blessed Mannes, brother of St. Dominic, the monastery church was built in 1234, the year of Dominic's canonization. The Moors sacked the surrounding districts in the second half of the thirteenth century, but Calaroga was far enough removed from the battle front to be spared from their plundering, and its castle served as a refuge to the rural inhabitants.

Calaroga is not located in the desert like section of Castile, but in a region of great fertility. The estates of the royal house of Guzman stretched over many miles. In the latter half of the twelfth century the castle was occupied by a descendant of the Guzman family, Felix, who in his youth had fought in the victorious army; now in peacetime his concern as landlord was that Castile should again deserve the title, "Granary of Europe." His wife Joanna, daughter of the Count of Aza, was his equal in nobility of birth and refinement of character. Of their several children three became priests. Anthony, a diocesan priest, dedicated his saintly life to works of charity in a hospital. Another son, Mannes, joined his younger brother Dominic in the Preaching Order in 1215. He assisted in establishing the Order in Paris, annexed the convent in Madrid to the Order of Friars Preachers, and left a permanent monument to his brother's honor by erecting a church at his birthplace, Calaroga. Mannes himself is venerated in Spain and throughout the Dominican Order as a Blessed.

A singular vision preceded the birth of Dominic in 1170. In the vision, "It seemed to his mother," says Jordan of Saxony, "that she was carrying within her a dog who escaped holding in his mouth a flaming torch with which he set the world on fire." Disturbed by this vision, Joanna made a pilgrimage to the Benedictine Abbey of Silos, about twelve miles from Calaroga, to seek counsel at the tomb of the sainted Abbot Dominic, who had reformed the abbey in the first half of the twelfth century, and was at this period held in great renown as a miracle worker. Receiving the desired enlightenment, that she would give birth to a son who would enlighten the world by his preaching, she returned home and named the son who was born shortly afterward in honor of her benefactor, Dominic. It was a common enough name in Spain at that time. Among the Canons of Osma, Dominic later found two other priests bearing the same baptismal name. The first companion to follow the Founder of the Friars Preachers in southern France also bore the name Dominic with the surname, "The Spaniard." The name Dominic means, "Given by the Lord." With Joanna's dream in mind, later biographers designate Dominic as God's hound.

At Dominic's baptism his godmother is said to have seen a star illuminating his brow and bathing the world in its brightness; of course, devout ladies sometimes do see things which are more imaginary than real, but the fact that her vision has withstood eight centuries of careful weighing makes it worth our consideration. Tradition has taken such firm hold of both these stories that the dog and star have become a part of the Order's coat-of-arms and are usually shown in pictures of the Saint. The font used at Dominic's baptism is no longer in the church at Calaroga; on May 28, 1605, King Philip III ordered it moved to the Dominican Church in Valladolid, where it was used at the baptismal ceremony of his first son, performed by the Cardinal-Archbishop of Toledo. Later it was transferred to the Dominican Church in Madrid, where it is still often used in administering the sacrament of baptism.

Felix Guzman and Joanna of Aza were descendants of the Visigoths, who had inhabited Castile since 800. They mixed freely with the ordinary people, although by birth they belonged to the ruling class. In Dominic this Teutonic origin showed itself in his physical appearance. According to the testimony of Blessed Cecilia, who knew the Founder of the Friars Preachers personally and was closely associated with him, he was of medium height and slight build, his complexion somewhat ruddy, and his tonsure and beard a light red. Dominic's habit of forming an estimate of persons and events only after quiet and disinterested deliberation, and his firm and refined disposition, may be considered an inheritance from his virtuous mother; his keen intellect, sound judgment, and tenacious perseverance in carrying out his convictions probably came from his father, Felix.

We can imagine that as a boy, Dominic often climbed the old castle tower in order to explore the distant horizon. If this tower could speak, it would very probably relate the boyish plans of adventure that filled his mind when scanning the countryside. There would be unfolded to us the picture of a rather solemn boy, little interested in games, somewhat sensitive and impressionable, a delicately responsive person.

GUMIEL DE IZAN

Not far distant from Calaroga was the venerable old Cistercian Abbey of Gumiel de Izan. Dominic's maternal uncle was the archpriest of the parish church connected with the Abbey; and to him the boy was sent for his elementary education. Ordinarily this instruction was given by lay teachers, but close blood relationship between the archpriest and Dominic, and the desire that their son should receive sound religious training, no doubt prompted Felix and Joanna to send him there. Moreover, Joanna's premonitory dream and the godmother's vision made the parents feel that God had an unusual vocation charted out for this boy.

In Gumiel de Izan the remembrance of the young Dominic is preserved in a graphic manner, but in the parish church, not in the Cistercian Abbey, even though this institution was closely

connected with the Guzman family and sheltered
the vault where Dominic's ancestors were buried.
There is a magnificent painting above the altar
depicting the fifteen Rosary mysteries. But even
more interesting is the legend carved on a pillar
near the entrance. On this remarkable monument,
first noticed by P. J. Keller in 1895, it is related that
when Dominic was serving his reverend uncle's
Mass in the parish church, he suddenly broke into
hearty laughter, a most unusual action in the
naturally quiet and devout boy. After Mass the
astonished priest asked for an explanation. Very
naïvely Dominic told him that he had seen two
ladies speaking together excitedly. On the bench
behind them, leaning his back on the memorable
pillar, sat the devil, writing carefully on a
parchment scroll whatever the ladies were saying.
Not being able to unwind the scroll fast enough to
keep pace with their animated conversation, the
devil grabbed one end of the scroll with his fist, got
a firm hold of the other end between his teeth, and
pulled with all his might. The parchment suddenly
tore apart, and the devil's head cracked against the
pillar. "To see the devil hurting himself and unable
to continue writing struck me funny. That is why
I laughed during Mass."

With the completion of his elementary
studies and the acquisition of rudimentary Latin,
Dominic's twelve-year stay in Gumiel de Izan came
to an end. When the time for leave-taking was at
hand, for the last time he visited his ancestors'
tombs in the Cistercian Abbey. Here the voices of

the departed spoke to him of the transitoriness of everything earthly. If any inordinate desires for honors or possessions lurked in his soul, they were quickly and forever put in order by this farewell visit to his dead forefathers. Having already decided not to spend his life grasping for money, pleasure, or power, this visit served him as the occasion for a complete breaking loose from everything earthly. The Master's invitation, "If thou wilt be perfect, go sell what thou hast and give to the poor" (Mt. 19:21), did not depress Dominic as it had the rich young man in the Gospel. His only sadness was that he could not answer Christ's invitation immediately.

In his farewell visit to the stately church his memory dwelt devoutly on his First Holy Communion and the many feast days when he had been permitted to receive his Lord. A glance at the altar recalled the many holy Masses he had served. As if to relive all these sacred occasions, he knelt for a long time in prayer. Finally he retraced his steps to the rectory, said good-by to his priest-uncle, and murmured appreciation for all the benefits bestowed on him, especially for the example of true priestliness in everyday life. This uncle had been to him not merely an instructor in the elements of knowledge, but also a father and leader in the spiritual life who had extended and deepened the spirituality implanted in his heart by Joanna. Perhaps Dominic gulped hard, as boys still do when trying to check unwelcome tears, when his hand was clasped a last time in those of his spiritual father. Then he set his footsteps toward Calaroga.

PALENCIA

At the close of the twelfth century the city of Palencia was the seat of the most illustrious college in Castile. The city had long been a bishopric. In 730 the Moors had destroyed much of its ancient splendor, but King Sancho the Great restored it in 1035. The importance of this college, connected with the cathedral, is proved by the fact that King Alphonsus VIII raised it to a University in 1212. Within its walls the arts, philosophy, and theology were taught together with canon law. It is unknown whether the episcopal city of Osma, to whose jurisdiction Calaroga belonged, did not possess a theological seminary at this time or if the fame of Palencia's College attracted Dominic, but at any rate we know that he enrolled among Palencia's students in 1189. The priesthood was his goal. This choice corresponded with the signs that had accompanied his birth and baptism, and with the desires and expectations of his devout parents, especially his mother, but it was above all the result of his own decision.

The journey to Palencia marked a decided change in Dominic's life. His first seven years had been spent in a quiet household; the companionship of his older brothers had filled his childhood with talk of the priesthood and accustomed him to the studious side of life. The twelve years in his uncle's presbytery did not give him a much broader sky line. A world hitherto unknown to the boy was opened before him on his arrival in Palencia; the new surroundings held peculiar dangers. Judged by twelfth-century standards, Palencia was a large city. Within its walls lived a population made up of the most varied elements. Here, as in every city, not only the rich and the poor walked side by side, but saints and thugs rubbed elbows. Students from all territories of Catholic Spain flocked to Palencia to perfect themselves in logic, grammar, rhetoric, and languages, and they became as fluent in Latin as in their mother tongue. At the same seat of knowledge others sought to penetrate the problems of philosophy, so as to be armed for the intellectual warfare against the Arabian philosophers, who gloried in their acquaintance with all the Greek sages, especially Aristotle. Here were assembled the future politicians, lawyers, magistrates, and senators, who would later attack the nation's social and political problems. Theological students studied Holy Writ and the Works of the Fathers and compiled their notes from Peter the Lombard, as directed by the professors in preparation for their future task of explaining the truths of Christianity in words simple enough for the ordinary person to understand. Because desire for knowledge is not always impelled by the purest motives, it is not surprising that among this student body were some whose ideals were not praiseworthy, and that not all were morally strong enough to resist the lure of worldliness.

In this university the nineteen-year-old Dominic enrolled, but the excitement of city life and collegiate surroundings failed to jostle him out of his love of silence and study. We do not know if a mentor accompanied him, as was often true with the sons of nobility, but all evidence serves to strengthen the opinion that his parents trusted him implicitly and allowed him to begin his new career unattended. Dominic did not take lodging in a dormitory, but, as we learn from an observation in his memorandum, he boarded with a private family. During his stay in Palencia he strove with firm and continuous conviction toward his chosen ideal, the attainment of a university degree and admission to ecclesiastical orders. The same diligence with which he had studied the fundamentals of knowledge while in his uncle's rectory was kept up in his search after higher knowledge. Even if at this early age Dominic did not fully realize his future vocation, he nevertheless felt obliged to take advantage of everything which would be necessary or useful in the life of a priest. In the first two years at the University of Palencia Dominic acquired such proficiency in the Latin language that he could debate freely with scholars of all lands, while his fluency in French and Italian enabled him later to preach to the people of these countries. The current needs of Spain urged him to devote two additional years to the study of philosophy, so as to be able to refute the errors of Arabian and Jewish philosophers. Such names as Ibn Sina, Al-Gazzali, and Ibn Roschd were not unknown to him. He learned about the efforts of these men and their disciples, enemies of Christianity, how they used their false system of knowledge to attack the truths of an almighty God, the immortality of the soul, predestination, and human freedom. An ardent determination was aroused in Dominic, the student of philosophy, someday to bring these enemies of Christianity to bay and to instruct and lead them back to the true faith. Consequently he called upon all his energies in order to acquire a clear perception of these intricate problems, which would enable him to distinguish accurately between falsehood and truth. But philosophy is a dry study, and we may suppose that Dominic did not find much personal satisfaction in it, even if his keen intellect moved easily in this rarefied mental atmosphere and he rejoiced at every successively deeper insight into truth and each new argument in confirmation of the natural law.

Philosophy, the study of the causes of all phenomena of mind and matter, is an abstruse subject. It is only the person of exceptional intelligence who picks up a philosophical book to read for entertainment. Students for the priesthood being made of the same ordinary clay as the rest of mankind, it is not surprising that the years devoted to philosophy are difficult for them, and that sometimes even the noblest minded are tempted to doubt their vocation. This does not seem to have been the case with Dominic.

The successful completion of philosophy marks the beginning of theology, the science that treats of the existence, nature, and attributes of God. The satisfaction Dominic found in theological studies was an additional proof that he had chosen the right state of life. The income of a benefice had no allurements for one who had already decided to renounce his inheritance and embrace absolute poverty. He was becoming more and more convinced that God was calling him to His service in the sanctuary and to the work of saving souls. To this calling he brought a clear intellect, strong will, undivided heart, inviolable body; knowing that these qualities are as brittle as glass, Dominic preserved them by following a rigorous program of prayer, fasting, and mortification. One of his penitential practices, total abstinence from wine, does not seem so extraordinary until we recall that in the Spain of Dominic's time, and even today in some European countries, wine was as much a part of every meal as coffee is at the American table. In the Guzman home wine was given even to the servants and beggars. The outstanding miracle in the life of Dominic's mother revolves around a wine cask which she had emptied in supporting the poor, and which she afterward found replenished by Divine Providence.

Textbooks and shelves of reference books were unknown before the invention of mechanical printing. The closest thing to a theology textbook was the Sentences of Lombard. These brief guiding points Dominic elaborated with notes taken from his professors' lectures. He also possessed what in those days was considered an unusual aid to learning, a few manuscripts, which he had bought at a high price. Reflection on the lectures and recalling and memorizing the important points indicated by his notes, occupied the free hours of his days and also many hours of the nights. If the study of philosophy had often perplexed his thoughts and confused his mind because of the many contradictory views and opinions set forth, so that his soul found therein scanty nourishment, in theology quite the contrary occurred. Here were expounded truths with which he had long been familiar and upon which he had fashioned his life and framed his attitude toward creation; now these principles were being deepened, widened, and began to exert a more energetic influence over his interior and exterior life.

All respectable twelfth-century students were expected to assist at the entire liturgical Office either in the Cathedral or in a Monastery Church on Sundays and feast days, the Office beginning with Matins at midnight and ending with Compline the following evening. Blessed Jordan tells us that the psalmody of the choir and monks exercised such an influence on the student Dominic that his whole life took on a spiritual flavor.

Two incidents mentioned in the canonization process to prove Dominic's heroic charity belong to his student years. Because of a poor harvest and the limited means of transportation, a serious famine arose in Castile. Palencia was hard hit. Dominic shared his food and money with others. When these were used up, he sold his precious and irreplaceable manuscripts in order to help the poor. The rebuke of imprudence he answered with the observation: "How could I study from dead skins when living skins are dying of hunger!" At another time Dominic heard of a poor woman whose brother, the wage earner of the family, had been captured by the Moors. Lacking the ransom money, Dominic offered to take the prisoner's place. There is no reason to doubt that he would have done so had not another way of freeing the man been found. These two incidents tell us that his austerity and love of study did not render him insensible to the sufferings of others.

Although we have few details of Dominic's student years, the fact that in later years he was a cheerful and sociable priest, able to mix with the people without losing his priestly decorum, warrants the statement that he was an ideal student. The seminarian is father of the priest. The accuracy of mind demanded of him by these years of philosophical and theological studies steadied, strengthened, and settled his compassionate nature. His adaptability to his surroundings and his ready understanding of another's misfortune produced in him that evenness of character which is frequently mentioned in the canonization process.

OSMA

Osma, one of Castile's oldest cities, lies at

the juncture of two rivers, the Avian and Ucero. It was made a bishopric in the seventh century. The Moors plundered the city, and the episcopal throne seems to have been vacant between 888 and 1088. When the Moors evacuated this territory, Osma soon recovered its former status, and in 1175 Bishop Prudentius obliged the cathedral canons to live a community life and serve the smaller city or country parishes which were too poor to support a regular pastor. While it is true that this reform was short-lived, yet when Bishop Martin Bazan, who succeeded Bishop Prudentius in 1189, made his canonical visitation, he could refer to this obligation of his chapter to live in community according to the Rule of St. Augustine. Some of the canons, among them Diego de Azevedo, gladly agreed to the proposal. But because other members disagreed, the Bishop decided upon a slower, but more effective method of reform; in the future he accepted only those priests into the Cathedral Chapter who had previously vowed to live in community according to the Rule of St. Augustine. He kept a close watch on the junior clergy and candidates for ordination. Diego, who by then had become a consultor, directed the attention of his Bishop toward the theology student, Dominic. Although at this time studying at Palencia, Dominic belonged to the diocese of Osma. The Bishop knew of Dominic's high rating as a scholar, his regularity at the Divine Office on the prescribed days, and his practical charity toward the poor. In 1195 Dominic received Holy Orders and was admitted into the Cathedral Chapter of Osma. He made profession according to the Rule of St. Augustine and was thereafter obligated to the Church of Osma as a canon regular.

Why did Dominic choose this rather uninteresting way of life? His mother's prophetic vision and his own baptismal name pointed toward the Benedictine Abbey at Silos; it seems that Dominic had often stayed there for intervals. Family tradition was directed to Gumiel de Izan, where his ancestors were buried and where the Cistercians lived in the spirit of St. Bernard. In the Premonstratensian Abbey of La Vid, only a few miles from Calaroga, the sons of St. Norbert combined the solemn liturgical functions with parochial work. He could also have followed the example of his two brothers and served the Church as a diocesan priest. In the light of Dominic's future life, we may safely say that he did not accept Bishop Martin's invitation blindly, just because he was asked, but that he fully realized the reason of the request. The Bishop was looking to him for energetic support in reforming not only his Chapter, but the entire diocese. Within the year following Dominic's entrance into the Chapter, it was transformed into a regular Augustinian Monastery. Diego was elected Prior and Dominic, then only twenty-six years old, Subprior. The electors must have seen unusual qualities in this young priest.

An Augustinian Canon's first obligation is the solemn chant of the Divine Office. The day hours are interrupted by the various divisions of the Office: Prime at six, Terce at nine, Sext at eleven, None at three, Vespers at five, and Compline at seven. In a well-ordered monastery everything goes as if by clockwork; obedience to rules and superiors is the firm foundation of peace and regularity; and the best contribution an individual religious can make to his community is to spread the infection of good example. As Subprior Dominic's duty was twofold: to be the first in obedience to the Prior's orders and the established rules, and in the Prior's absence to take his place as head of the house. We know little of Dominic's days at Osma except that he followed an even round of life, assembling with the others to chant the Office and quitting the cloister precincts only when accompanying the Bishop on official business; but we may safely conjecture that mixing with the canons, many of them young like himself, brought out his latent good qualities. It was really the first time he associated intimately with people of his own age; at home he had been the youngest, at his uncle's presbytery a mere boy, and at Palencia he found his books more interesting than his companions and shrank from their frivolous amusements. Now as Subprior he conquered the timidity of boyhood; and as Blessed Jordan says, "appeared among his brother canons as a ray of sunshine, in humility the least, in holiness the first, shedding around him an aroma of quickening life, like the fragrance of pinewoods on a hot summer day." In his Rule, St. Augustine says that community life is like a building, with love of God as the foundation and fraternal charity the supporting pillars; perhaps the reason of Dominic's popularity was the charity and respect he showed to all.

Bishop Martin was satisfied with the young Subprior, but Prior Diego was a little worried about one thing. Dominic wasn't eating enough, and abstained entirely from wine. So he took his Subprior aside and gave him some fatherly advice, as the Apostle Paul in his first letter to Timothy reproved his disciple. The Prior told Dominic to give up his abstaining from wine — that his health did not permit it. He requested the Subprior to drink the customary glass of wine and assured him that it would make him vigorous. Dominic followed this counsel, although he diluted the wine freely with water. The experienced Prior valued this obedience much more than the former austerity.

Bishop Martin Bazan died in 1201. He could close his eyes peacefully because his Cathedral Chapter had been reformed in accordance with the recommendation of the Council of Mayence (813). Diego's appointment as his successor left the office of Prior vacant. It seems but natural that Dominic would have been elected to fill the vacancy, but he continued as Subprior. The reason for this was not due to a change of opinion among the canons. They had chosen him as Subprior and were well satisfied with their choice. They would now have elected him as Prior if he himself had not pleaded with them not to vote for him, but to select an older canon for that post.

Bishop Diego was not disappointed at the outcome of the election. On the contrary he took it as a run of luck because it enabled the old friendly relations to continue. The direction of the Chapter claimed the entire attention of the Prior, but the Subprior the Bishop could appoint to various services without detriment to discipline. If Diego made a visitation of his parishes, called at the royal palace in the interests of his diocese, or consecrated a new church, Dominic was usually seen at his side. This well-balanced life of prayer and activity continued for eight years. It was the divinely supplied period for the young priest to study and strengthen his own character. The years ahead were to be devoted to exterior organization and administration; to do this successfully his own interior had first to be set in order and brought under control.

II
IN THE RETINUE OF BLESSED DIEGO

THE AQUITANIAN JOURNEY

AT THE beginning of the thirteenth century the Castilian and French royal families were closely related, but King Alphonse VIII of Castile wanted to form an even closer alliance with France, so he decided on a marriage between his son Ferdinand and the daughter of a certain French lord, whose name we are not told. Bishop Diego of Osma was appointed to negotiate this project. On the King's part, this choice was a sign of his confidence in the Bishop. Diego, as was his custom, asked Subprior Dominic to accompany him on this journey. This request implied more than just a summons to be companion on diocesan visitations. Here there was question of a weighty family concern of the Royal House, a matter of no little importance for the entire kingdom. The two set out with appropriate equipage and escort. As royal ambassador, Diego must appear with royal splendor. As Bishop, Diego was accompanied by a number of distinguished clerics. The king had supplied him with a bodyguard of knights and mounted troops. There were also the workmen to look after the luggage-laden mules.

The oldest historians give no more precise

details than that the journey was made to the
Aquitanian Boundary, because King Alphonse had
decided on a marriage between his son, Ferdinand,
and the daughter of a certain "Lord of the
Marches." The shortest and safest route for this trip
would have been the road along the seashore, but
because Toulouse was the first stop in France, it is
generally thought that Diego and his suite took
instead the road leading over the mountains. They
traveled upstream on the Noguera, climbed the
barren slopes of the Upper Pyrenees, passed by the
bleak, rugged walls of the Maladetta, forced their
way through the Pass de Rios, arrived at the
Garonne district, and descended into one of the
most beautiful and fertile sections of Europe, the
fruitful and delightful territory of southern France,
their journey's destination. They had passed
through sharply contrasting landscapes, from
rough plateaus through stony headlands, along
rugged mountainsides and past high waterfalls in
that land so lavishly bedecked by nature, the
charming country of the Troubadours. Physically it
was a passage from difficult to pleasant; morally it
was leaving the society of the men of firm religious
conviction who belonged to the Cathedral Chapter
and mixing with devotional weaklings, blown here
and there by every wind of heretical doctrine.

There was not much communication
between France and Spain at this time except
official intercourse. Perhaps some news about the
latest heresy sprouting up in southern France had
seeped into Spain, but of what interest was that to

the Spaniards, who had torn every inch of their own country from Christianity's worst foe? Diego and Dominic were soon to meet an adherent of this heresy in Toulouse. The innkeeper of the hostelry where they lodged their first night in France had fallen away from the church and joined the Albigensians, but he gave hospitality to the distinguished travelers and saw that no convenience was wanting to them. Diego and the retinue were tired and hurried to bed. Dominic and the innkeeper remained in the dining room.

During his night watches before the tabernacle at Osma, Dominic had imbibed Christ's own compassion for sinners. He now sat face to face with one of the most unfortunate, a man more miserable than even the Moors, because he had abandoned the happiness they had never possessed. In Dominic compassion was united with the urge to lead back to the faith this man, whom he had never seen before and would probably never see again. The innkeeper felt attracted to this cheerful, gracious stranger, whose clothing, after the traveling cloak had been laid aside, marked him as a priest. The clerical appearance opened the door for the Albigensian to speak about the "Perfect," as the traveling Albigensian preachers were called, whose poor and austere life contrasted so sharply with the relaxed morals of many Catholic priests. They fasted rigorously and encouraged sinners by the consoling doctrine of eternal happiness without penance in the present life, or purgatory or hell hereafter. He discoursed also on the opposition between good and evil, between body and soul, between God and the devil, and finally rose to the accusation that all Catholic priests were the devil's spokesmen. A glance at his listener may have placed on his lips the self-correction that not quite all the clergy were included in that denunciation, but the great majority. Now it was Dominic's turn to speak. His thorough foundation in philosophy and theology served him well, but the man did not surrender his viewpoint without an argument. It got to be midnight; the discussion continued, the Albigensian accusing, Dominic rectifying. Morning dawned. The heretic had presented all his points, only to have them blasted one after another. Now there was no other alternative for him than to admit that he had lived in error. Dominic had reclaimed him to the true faith. This apostolic night watch was the most decisive in Dominic's life. At Osma he had prayed and done penance for the conversion of sinners, but here his words had persuaded a fallen-away Catholic to turn over a new leaf.

Early in the morning the travelers were on their way to Aquitaine, where Diego broached his ruler's request and received a favorable reply. The purpose of the journey was thereby accomplished and the travelers returned to Spain. If Diego hoped that the king would free him from further services upon the successful outcome of this embassy and permit him to return to his bishopric, he was headed for a disillusionment. King Alphonse believed that because Diego had been so quick and expert in the first half of the project, no better man could be found to complete it. So the same company soon retraced their steps to Aquitaine, this time charged to escort the future bride to Castile. No details of this trip are mentioned, only the futility of the enterprise: the princess died before their arrival. Diego did not return immediately to Spain, but sent a messenger with the death information. He decided to make the most of the journey and go to Rome in order to consult the Pope on some personal business. Dominic was his companion on this Rome-bound trip. The unexpected death of the princess had impressed him deeply, as it had affected all the royal embassy; but more lasting was the impression made on his soul during that momentous night when God had used him as an instrument in reclaiming an erring soul.

CITEAUX

Bishop Diego is an interesting character, an impressionable Spaniard of Celtic descent. He was not one of those worldly-minded prelates so sadly numerous in medieval church history, but a bishop with God's glory at heart. He knew that King Alphonse VIII was planning a fresh Crusade order to overthrow the Moors and liberate the Christians suffering under Islam's dominion. Diego could not disapprove of the plan, for the Pope himself was in favor of it; but Diego preferred a peaceful missionary enterprise among the Moors, who still occupied a large part of Spain. Of course, he fully realized that this undertaking was fraught with serious dangers because the Moors, no matter how broad-minded their leaders professed to be, would not tolerate the open propagation of Christianity in their territory. In spite of this, Diego was determined to make the attempt. He had often discussed this plan with his Subprior at Osma and was sure of his co-operation. The journey to Aquitaine was for both men an occasion to direct their steps toward Rome. Diego wanted to present his plan to the Pope, without whose consent he could not leave his bishopric for any length of time. Innocent III received the Bishop kindly, but abruptly refused the petition to resign his office as Bishop of Osma in order to convert the Moors. In his refusal the Pope was undoubtedly motivated by the conviction that a peaceful apostolate would bear no results at this particular time.

On his way back to Osma, Diego visited Citeaux on the Burgundian bank of the Saone, the most illustrious monastery of that period. Here St. Robert had effected the Cistercian reform and from it, by means of the General Chapters, the discipline of the individual houses was supervised. Citeaux had become a pilgrimage place for many Christians. Some went there to be edified by the holy lives of the monks, others to test their own vocation, and yet others to seek counsel in life's perplexities from these men who were accustomed to consider all problems in the light of eternity. Diego, true to his sanguine temperament, had expected the Pope to agree heartily with his plans. The refusal had so depressed him that his spiritual equilibrium was shaken. At Citeaux he hoped to steal a few words of consolation and encouragement from one of these perpetually silent men. The Abbot was away at the time, but Diego obtained the renewed zest he had hoped for; indeed, he was so impressed by the life of the monks that he quickly recovered from the disappointment experienced in Rome and became enkindled with a fresh project.

These white-robed monks, heads covered with high capuche, hands hidden in the spacious folds of sleeves, walking through the dimly lighted cloisters on the way to Matins during the night's deep silence, seemed to him as though living on a spiritual plateau, elevated high above the confusions and troubles of ordinary mortals. The solemn celebration of the Divine Office by this assembly of devout men seemed to him all-powerful in obtaining God's blessings. Diego decided to ask the Pope to permit him to become a Cistercian monk; but this request was likewise refused. So Diego had to be content with being clothed in St. Bernard's habit as an Oblate and receiving several monks into his retinue, who should plant the Order in his own diocese. This may seem like passing from one extreme to another, but the thing the sanguine Bishop was attempting was not a crossing of extremes, but of uniting mutually exclusive ideals, contemplation and activity. Dominic, his trusted companion, did not join the Bishop in this attempt to become a Cistercian Monk. He remained a Canon of Osma for the time being, but later on succeeded in removing the antagonistic elements from these two ideals and uniting their essential qualities into a new standard. This was to be the inheritance he would bestow upon his followers.

MONTPELLIER

Diego and Dominic did not return immediately to Osma when leaving Citeaux. They made a detour into southern France so as to meet the Abbot of Citeaux at Montpellier.

By the reception of the Cistercian habit, Diego had become the Abbot's spiritual son. This made it his duty to visit him and give him an account of his sojourn in the abbey. The Pope had appointed Abbot Arnold and two monks, Peter of Castelnau and Raoul of Fontfroide, to work at the conversion of the Albigensians. Fickleness seems to have been the outstanding trait of the Albigensians, who had in turn been Catholics, Gnostics, and Manicheans. In the twelfth century the Albigensian heresy took deep root in the soil of southern France, already well cultivated by religious upheavals.

Strictly speaking, Albigensianism was not a new heresy, but a revival of the old pagan theory of two supreme beings, matter and spirit. Matter was said to be essentially evil and spirit essentially good. According to this doctrine, God was the author of everything spiritual; the devil, of everything material. Matter, they said, was the evil creation of an evil spirit, and so every living thing was unclean and physical life the greatest misfortune. To propagate or prolong human life were evil acts; murder and suicide were acts of goodness. Marriage was considered the curse of the world, because it propagated human life; the divine maternity of the Blessed Virgin, being an example of woman's part in the production of evil, was held in derision. Anything that lessened the vigor of the human body was highly commendable, so excessive fasting, complete abstinence from flesh meat and wine, fanatical disciplines, lacerated and half-starved bodies, were the proof of inner holiness. Since bread and wine were said to be creations of the devil, the Albigensians treated the Blessed Sacrament as an abomination. The holding of property, by the Church or anyone else, was considered essentially wrong, and the Catholic papacy, bishops, and priests were the devil's go-betweens.

In order to understand the appeal such a doctrine could offer to the masses, we need but remember that falsehood always disguises itself in attractive garb. Only the "Perfect," a select minority, were obliged to virginity, absolute poverty, and ascetic practices; all that was asked of the rest of the crowd was to reject the Catholic faith and to renounce belief in the sacraments, because these were based on material signs. The heretics flattered every class of society; the rich were promised a share in the spoils of the Church's possessions, and working men were given a free opportunity to learn a trade in workshops conducted by the "Perfect." Although marriage was considered a great sin, by a strange inconsistency the Albigensians declared that sexual passions must be satisfied, and concubinage was no worse than marriage. There was only one sacrament, the "consolamentum," to be received at the moment of death; but even if a person died without receiving it, he was not doomed to eternal suffering because there was neither hell nor purgatory. Perhaps it was this "consolamentum," the promise of eternal happiness no matter how evil a man's earthly life, that gave the heresy its greatest attraction.

It is undeniable that the Albigensian seed would never have taken such deep root if there had not been a deplorable relaxation among the Catholic clergy, many of whom were more concerned about personal comfort and wealth than the purity of faith or souls to be saved. Pope Innocent III had to depose several bishops for heresy. The majority of priests were lacking in zeal and solid instruction; their life was worldly and immoral. There was a mad scramble whenever a rich benefice became vacant. The small minority of zealous priests and bishops only served to make the scandal of the lax more obnoxious, as a lone star accentuates the darkness of a cloudy night.

Pope Innocent III, whose vision was as broad as it was practical, recognized the danger to civil and religious peace hidden in this insidious doctrine. He commissioned the Cistercians, one of the strictest Orders in the Church, to preach against the heresy. The Abbot of Citeaux was put in charge of the enterprise and two of the monks, Peter and Raoul, were made papal legates. The Cistercian vocation is to a life of prayer and solitude. None of these monks had been trained in the art of disputation, so the Abbot thought to make up for this deficiency by surrounding the preaching monks with the external pomp which canon law permits to papal legates. This was like throwing more fuel into the fire of the Albigensian preachers. It was plainly evident that a spectacular mass conversion was impossible under these circumstances. Abbot Arnold and the two papal legates, weary and discouraged, had met at Montpellier in order to discuss what was to be done.

The eyes of Diego and Dominic had been wide open during their three previous journeys through this region. Dominic's conversion of the innkeeper had convinced them that one nail must be driven out by another, false sanctity by real sanctity, preaching lies by preaching truth. Now they came to the same district for the fourth time. Arrived at Montpellier, Diego told Abbot Arnold of his investiture in the Cistercian habit. The Abbot and the two legates were so impressed by the Bishop's fervor that they confided their despondency in the Albigensian struggle to him. Diego, who had so recently been denied his request to evangelize the Moors, and shortly after had earnestly petitioned to enter the Cistercian Order, there to work for the conversion of mankind by prayer and penance, was now instantaneously fired anew with the first ideal. He related to the legates the incident of Dominic's conversion of the innkeeper, and the various observations they had made during their travels through this locality. Because the Albigensian preachers misled the people principally by means of their own penitential life and by pointing scornfully to the riches and comfortable life of the Catholic clergy, merely expounding the truths of Christianity would obtain no results. Here example must be placed against example. Hypocritical virtue must be overcome by true Christian virtue. Diego admitted that, as ambassadors of the Pope, the legates had the right to travel with external display. Under certain circumstances, such a procedure might even be obligatory; but here such grandeur would defeat the very purpose of the enterprise. Because the Albigensian preachers traversed the countryside barefooted, comparing the Church and her possessions to Satan's synagogue, it was necessary to lay aside all exterior magnificence. If love of God was the motivating force in this life of poverty, Diego reasoned, success would surely follow. This doctrine sounded strange to Abbot Arnold, honored in all Christendom. The two legates admitted the logic of the proposal, but doubted the possibility of carrying it out. In order to convince them, the impetuous Diego volunteered to join them in the enterprise if the legates agreed to the proposal. This they did. As for Dominic, he seems to have had no premonition that he was to remain twelve years in southern France after the end of the Crusade to continue the peaceful system of conversion, or that he was to found an Order which would spread from France throughout the world. Nevertheless, these events were be as a crowning finale of that fateful night watch he had spent with his Albigensian host at Toulouse.

MONTREAL

Abbot Arnold could not share in the execution of the proposed experiment. The General Chapter of the Cistercian Order was due shortly, so he had to return to Citeaux and make the necessary preparations; but he promised to recruit fresh laborers for the missionary field from the assembled Abbots. Peter of Castelnau promised to take part. The attempt would not be easy for him. In 1199, while Peter was Canon of Maguelonne, Pope Innocent had appointed him Legate. In 1202 he entered the Cistercian Order, but in the following year the Pope again chose him as Legate. Peter was a high-spirited man, never recoiling from difficult measures if he felt they were necessary. He had obtained the deposition of the heretical Bishop of Beziers and had excommunicated several princes who refused to join the struggle against the Albigensians. When these measures did not obtain the desired results, he presented to Rome his resignation of the office of Legate in order to retire to a monastery. In reply Innocent told him that now was not the time to enjoy the peace of the cloister, but to labor for the conversion of the heretics. Thereafter Peter remained at his post and decided to join in the new project. But he was soon to realize that his former stern methods were a stumbling block for the present plan. The other Legate, Raoul, was a prayerful, patient man, a suitable companion for Diego and Dominic.

Following Diego's example, the Legates dismissed their attendants and then traveled about on foot, preaching whenever and wherever an opportunity presented itself; but the austerity of their life was more convincing than any sermon. Many of the Catholic clergy had secretly accepted the Albigensian doctrines without separating themselves openly from the Church. These now became attentive and some decided that it was better to stay with the old Church, which had for many centuries commanded the same discipline by means of which these innovators were trying to allure people away from her. As for Diego and Dominic, everybody knew that these Spaniards had sacrificed their homeland in order to carry out a difficult, thankless work. The Albigensian leaders admitted that their moral rectitude and bodily austerity eclipsed their own, and deplored the fact that they did not belong to the Cathari, the Pure.

Montpellier, with its surrounding countryside, was the first missionary field where the new method was tried with a modicum of success. At Beziers, Peter of Castelnau experienced the bitter consequences of his former methods. The people mistrusted him; in their opinion his exterior poverty was merely a pretext. Because of him the other missionaries were also refused a favorable hearing, so Peter was requested to withdraw. He did so, but was from then on so convinced of the inefficiency of the new method that he began to urge a fresh Crusade. His companion, Raoul, remained with Diego and Dominic.

The missionary preachers exposed the Albigensian errors whenever and wherever they could get a hearing, in the open squares, public buildings, or in churches. Their discourses were consequently regarded not as sermons, but as lectures or disputations. In 1206 Diego held such a disputation at Servian with the former Canon of Nevers who had joined the Albigensians, changed his name from William to Theodoric, and was now in high favor among the heretics. Diego's knowledge and enthusiasm caused his astonished opponent to acknowledge: "I know what spirit animates you. You are come in the spirit of Elias!" But because Theodoric would not admit that this confession would logically lead him to return to the Catholic faith, Diego exclaimed in the hearing of the dumfounded audience: "If I am come in the spirit of Elias, then you are animated with the spirit of anti-Christ!" Although no definite result was achieved as far as the disputants were concerned, the people seem to have favored Diego and Dominic, because they gave them a formal escort when leaving the city.

A second public disputation took place at Montreal in October, 1206. It was the most important session which Diego had so far conducted. The Albigensians had invited him to attend this meeting the previous summer. The following conditions had been agreed to: assurance of safe conduct and a tribunal for debate composed of two representatives of each party who were to demonstrate their tenets solely from Holy Scripture, so that whichever side could not prove its views from that source alone would be considered the loser. The Albigensians presented three topics for discussion: Holy Mass, the Church, and the hierarchy. The first public assembly took place October 1, 1206, in the market place at Montreal. Albigensians from all the surrounding district crowded the market place. The disputation was limited to the first topic. Diego argued from Holy Writ against the Albigensian leader, Arnold Hot, by pointing out that Consecration, the central point of Holy Mass, is no invention of man but the arrangement of Jesus Christ, because at the Last Supper He Himself pronounced the words of consecration and commanded the Apostles to do likewise. No decision was reached at this meeting, but it was decided that each party would write out its proofs and after reciprocal examination a second disputation would be held toward the end of the month. Even then the question remained open, each party claiming the victory; but the reputation of the Albigensians was shaken because during the weeks which Diego and Dominic spent in Montreal following this event, they received nearly two hundred lapsed Catholics back into the Church.

At this time the missionaries also received reinforcements. True to his word, Abbot Arnold had persuaded several Abbots to come to their assistance. These fresh recruits accepted the new methods, showed a willing spirit, and endured patiently the hardships of poverty and hard work. Through their efforts many Catholics were strengthened in the faith, but among the heretics they were less successful; it seemed as though they could not match the crafty heretics in this war of wits.

In the following year a private conference took place between Diego and Durandus of Huesca in the castle of Count Raymond Roger. As a result of this conference Durandus returned to the Catholic Church from which he had apostatized in order to join the Waldensians. This conversion climaxed Diego's missionary labors. During the period in which the Bishop had directed the project, Dominic had joined in the preaching, disputation and writing out of theses; but in deference to his superior and senior he had kept himself in the background. In the time to come, as the situation became increasingly difficult, he was destined to take the lead.

PROUILLE

In the summer of 1207 Diego returned to his

diocese to take care of the needs of his flock. It was not his intention to remain in Osma but only to attend to the most urgent affairs and then return to France, there to continue his peaceful missionary labors among the Albigensians. In November, 1206, Diego had experienced the great satisfaction of knowing that Pope Innocent III, after listening to Raoul's report, had approved the new missionary project and commissioned the Legate to recruit more laborers. Such men being few and far between in heresy-cankered France, Diego intended to look around in Spain. As Diego covered the last miles of the difficult journey over the Pyrenees and entered his episcopal city, he was unaware of the fact that in the hardships of the trip he had contracted the germ of his last illness. He began to set diocesan affairs in order with even more than his usual zeal. By the end of November the symptoms could no longer be ignored, and on December 30 Diego died. Because of his heroic life and the many miraculous cures which took place at his tomb in the Cathedral Church at Osma, Rome beatified him and approved his liturgical veneration in the Cistercian Order and in the diocese of Osma. Members of the Dominican Order remember him as the paternal friend of their Founder and are grateful to him for the project which, in co-operation with Dominic, he began in southern France. Although the idea of a peaceful missionary conquest first took form in Dominic's mind after he had reclaimed a heretic as a result of a nightlong discussion, it required Diego's episcopal authority to submit the plan to the legates, and his personal example to carry the project into execution. These were all remote, but necessary preparations for the foundation of the Order of Preachers. Without Diego, Dominic would perhaps not have been Founder of the Preaching Order.

When news of the Bishop's death reached southern France the missionaries became anxious about the future, because they realized that Diego had been the driving force of the whole enterprise. The Cistercians withdrew. Unfortunately, Legate Raoul died shortly after. Of all those who had joined the missionary enterprise he was the only one who had remained with Dominic. Now Dominic was alone. Who would have blamed him if under these circumstances he had forsaken the work and returned to his canonry? But there was Prouille, the Bishop's last undertaking. Diego's commission that Dominic succeed him in the management of the mission project ceased to be binding when the desertion of the co-workers left nothing to manage, but the charge to provide for Prouille continued. There dwelt the pious ladies, and there also his namesake, Dominic the Spaniard, who had brought the death notice, waited further assignment to continue his work. Dominic remained in France primarily for the sake of Prouille, but also because of the missionary project which he considered important enough to merit a fresh beginning.

Prouille was a solitary castle between

Toulouse and Carcassonne. At this time the castle was almost in ruins, and the adjoining chapel abandoned. The few peasants who had remained faithful Catholics attended church services in Fanjeaux. Upon this desolate spot Diego and Dominic had directed their attention in 1206, when they decided to attack the Albigensians from a different angle, equipped with their own methods. The two missionaries had long noticed how the heretics used the feminine forces in order to strengthen and disseminate their doctrines. This was especially true in Montreal, where schools and conventions were conducted by Albigensian women. Since the instructions were imparted gratis, and the schools provided free room and board, the attendance was great. Heresy was made so attractive that the children who were educated in these institutions were lost to the true faith. A Catholic counterpart was an imperative necessity.

Dominic had influenced several ladies to live a life of prayer and penance; some historians say he had converted them from heresy. Whatever the case, they were determined to prove that the Catholic Church can inspire its members to live a life that is even more austere than that of the Albigensian "Perfect." After Dominic spoke to them about the necessity of teaching and training the children whose faith was being endangered, they decided to serve the Church in this way. The next step was to acquire a suitable residence. Diego turned to the Bishop of Toulouse, in which diocese Prouille was located. Bishop Faulke had traversed

this vicinity as missionary before entering the
Cistercian Order, where his unusual talents and
virtues caused him to be raised to the abbacy and
appointed Bishop of Toulouse in 1205. It was his
duty to correct the abuses which his heretical
predecessor had introduced into the diocese. He
knew by personal experience of the need for
Catholic education and donated the buildings
necessary for the project. This was the beginning of
the Monastery of Prouille.

Diego had insisted that the missionaries live
in perfect poverty, entirely dependent on the
voluntary offerings of the faithful, but Prouille
could not be conducted on this principle. Dominic
was therefore harassed by financial worries. He
could not approach Bishop Faulke for assistance
because this prelate had found his diocese as poor
financially as it was spiritually. Moreover, since he
had donated the buildings, more could not be asked
of him. Dominic turned to Archbishop Berengar of
Narbonne and found him a friend in need.
Contemporary documents show that Archbishop
Berengar presented the parish church of St. Martin
in Limoux with all its tithes and other revenues to
the pious women whom Brother Dominic of Osma
had converted from heresy to a life of Christian
holiness. In the same year, 1207, he made another
donation. Thereafter the gifts ceased temporarily,
because of the war, but the gifts of the year 1211
made up for the four intervening years. As a result
of the friendship which Dominic had formed with
Simon de Montfort, the Count conferred generous

gifts upon the Prouille enterprise. This made it possible for Dominic to purchase the necessary land on which to build a larger monastery, so that regular monastic life began in 1211. Until then the Sisters had been guided by Dominic's verbal instructions, but now the Rule of St. Augustine, which Dominic himself observed, became the foundation of their religious life. By this time there were eighteen sisters in the community, subject to the Prioress, Wilhelmine. Dominic, who always referred to himself as a Canon of Osma, is mentioned in a document by Simon de Montfort as Prior of Prouille. He always retained deep interest in the spiritual and material welfare of Prouille and obtained subjects for the community.

After preaching at Fanjeaux in 1207, he was approached by a group of ladies who had been misled by the specious virtues of the Albigensians, but were now wavering in their conviction because of Dominic's preaching. "Servant of God," they said to him, "if what you preached today be true, we have long been deceived by the spirit of error, for we have believed the men whom you call heretics. We beseech you, pray that the Lord will make the true faith known to us." He repeated the statements formerly made in his sermon, and affirmed that they had been serving the devil. That was not too severe a statement because previously these same ladies had accepted the heretic's doctrine that the Catholic clergy were Satan's cupbearers. When the ladies smiled skeptically at this remark he offered to show them who it was they adhered to. Then there burst into the church a hideous black demon and circled around them for half an hour. At Dominic's command he disappeared through a window. That convinced the ladies. They returned to the true faith, several of them even wanted to consecrate themselves entirely to God. Dominic directed them to Prouille, where a life of strict enclosure had not impeded the community's charitable works. The school continued. In Fanjeaux and Limoux other such schools were opened and conducted by the Sisters.

III

PEACEFUL LABORS IN WARTIME

CARCASSONNE

THE seed of Dominic's efforts produced such a rich harvest in the Prouille undertaking that even Diego could not have expected more. But as an apostle he was a failure. A series of events made it seem as if God did not favor the missionary project. The two leaders of the enterprise, Diego and Raoul, were dead and the Cistercians had returned to their monastery. The civil authorities and even the Pope decided on a military crusade to exterminate the heretics. In 1207 the papal legate, Peter of Castelnau, excommunicated the apostate Count Raymond of Toulouse. In reprisal, one of the Count's squires assassinated the papal legate. When Pope Innocent III heard of the murder of his legate he publicly excommunicated Count Raymond, released his vassals from allegiance, and asked King John of England and Philip II of France to join in the Crusade. The peaceful missionary project really looked like a thing of the past, but in spite of unfavorable prospects Dominic kept at the task entrusted to him by Diego.

Dominic was not a man of harsh violence, he was not a friend of thumbscrews and the stake.

Even though he belonged to a knightly family and his ancestors had proved their heroism on the battlefield, Dominic was a priest and consequently a man of peace. He remembered Christ's advice to hotheaded Peter: "Put up again thy sword into its place, for all that take the sword shall perish with the sword" (Mt. 26:52). Dominic did not condemn the custom of attacking with military force those heretics who tried to propagate their doctrines by force: these men endangered civic peace which depended on unity of faith, and also menaced social order because they rebelled against lawful authority. Neither did he censure the Church's practice of delivering obstinate heretics to the secular courts for punishment. But he was not a friend of such measures. Dominic has unjustly been called the author of the Inquisition, the medieval Court of Justice which was concerned entirely with the judicial prosecution of heretics. This procedure antedates Dominic, and it is a calumny to attribute it to him. Dominic sought out the erring in the spirit of mercy and tried to lead them back to the true faith by means of instruction and example, prayer and penance. That he succeeded in thus reclaiming many of those with whom he came in contact is proved by contemporary records, especially in the depositions of the witnesses at his canonization process. He preferred this personal contact to public disputations. While Diego was still with the missionaries, Dominic left to him the task of group discussions; private instruction of individual souls was his specialty.

Two documents prove that on the rare occasions when Dominic reconciled open heretics with the Church by imposing on them a public penance, he did so in obedience to the papal legate. With express reference to the Cardinal Legate, it is stated: "We permit Brother Dominic, Canon of Osma, and humble servant of the Word, to reconcile Raymond William of Altaripa." At another time, applying to the plenipotence of Abbot Arnold of Citeaux, Apostolic Legate, Dominic received back into the fold of the Church the apostate Count Roger. He imposed upon the Count the penance of receiving the discipline in public from the parish priest on three Sundays or holydays, and to observe three forty days fasts during the year. He was to attend Mass daily and say a prescribed number of prayers, could not leave the town without permission, and had to give a monthly account of himself to the pastor. These are indeed hard conditions, but they reflect the laws and customs of that period. Dominic imposed these penalties, not in his own name but as representative of the Legate, to whom the penitent could always appeal for mitigation or remission.

During the years 1213 and 1214 Dominic acted as Vicar-General of the Bishop of Carcassonne, temporarily absent from his diocese. A court proceeding seems to have been pending at this time against certain violent heretics who refused Dominic's promise of pardon if they renounced their errors. Thereupon he delivered them to the secular court, where they received the death penalty. On the way to their execution Dominic pleaded with the judge to spare one of the condemned, assuring him that the man would be converted. The judge granted pardon. Raymond de Grossi, the pardoned criminal, changed his life and later entered the Dominican Order. This incident is a cue to Dominic's character; he had delivered the criminals to the civil court as a matter of duty, but the plea for pardon was the spontaneous act of his kindly nature.

Dominic accepted the office of Vicar-General for two reasons: it gave him an opportunity to serve the absent Bishop and it set his residence in Carcassonne, the headquarters of his friend, Simon de Montfort. The episcopal office Dominic repeatedly declined. When he was chosen in 1215 as Bishop of Conserans he refused on the principle that the missionary project and Prouille needed him. In the same way he turned down the bishopric of Beziers. Not as Bishop did he want to work, but as a poor itinerant preacher, a true follower of the Great Apostle Paul. At times Dominic worked alone, because William Claret was charged with the direction of Prouille and later accepted the pastorship of Limoux. Several other priests joined the undertaking, although none of them seem to have persevered. Prouille was their headquarters; Dominic was considered the superior of the group, but they were not bound to him by any vow. Anyone was free to leave at will.

Carcassonne had been the Crusaders' center

of operations since 1209. There was hardly a ghost of a chance of successful missionary labor in a district devastated by savagery and slaughter; terrible acts of ferocity and treachery were perpetrated by both sides so that the minds of both Catholics and heretics became more confused and embittered. The prospect of converting the Albigensians was becoming smaller day by day. Public disputations, such as Diego had held at Montreal, were forbidden. Even after the Catholic victory at Muret, peace was not established; but under the ensign of the Crusade many sought their private interests. Dominic continued his peaceful missionary labors, preaching whenever an opportunity was offered; he addressed words of encouragement to whomever he met. If the person was Catholic, he tried to strengthen his convictions; if it was an Albigensian, he gave him the arguments in favor of the true faith. If no opportunity to preach the Gospel presented itself, he turned to God in prayer, beseeching Him to let fall on mankind the dew of saving grace. In his profound conception of God's methods of conversion Dominic appreciated the value of suffering, as the following will prove.

It was noticed that he had a predilection for Carcassonne, and frequently went there prior to his appointment as Vicar-General, and long before Simon de Montfort set up his headquarters there. When asked why he so often and gladly went there, his answer was, "Because in Carcassonne I find suffering." He seldom directed his footsteps toward Toulouse, where the people patted him on the back. A converted Albigensian of Carcassonne tells us that before his conversion, he and many of the citizens would meet Dominic with jeers and hisses, and throw rubbish at him whenever he came to the city. Dominic accepted these insults patiently in expiation for the sins of the offenders, and offered them as his contribution to the bitter sufferings of his Redeemer, as St. Paul says: "Who now rejoice in my sufferings for you, to fill up those things which are wanting in the sufferings of Christ in my flesh for His body, which is the church" (Col. 1:24).

The purpose of the Albigensians in thus insulting and molesting Dominic was to dissuade him from visiting Carcassonne. They also openly threatened to kill him, but he calmly replied: "I am unworthy to receive the crown of martyrdom. I have done nothing to deserve such an honorable death." At another time they waited in ambush for him. He was aware of their designs but did not change his route. Instead, he began to sing when approaching the danger zone so that they would not miss him. They did not attack him, but asked him what he would have done if they had. He answered: "I would have begged you not to kill me instantly, but to hack me to pieces limb after limb, thus prolonging my torture. I would have pleaded with you to show me each butchered member and finally to tear out my eyes and let me die slowly, thus polishing up my martyr's crown." After this the heretics stopped threatening him, for it was useless trying to scare a man who was delighted at the very thought of death.

Remembering our Lord's exhortation: "So let your light shine before men that they may see your good works and glorify your Father who is in heaven" (Mt. 2: i6), Dominic used his bodily penances to convert the heretics. Seeing that several noble ladies of Toulouse had been deceived by the showy austerity of the wandering preachers and were in danger of apostasy, he decided to visit their homes. When they set meat before him and his companion, Dominic explained that they could not eat it because Lent had begun. Would they kindly serve them merely bread and water? The soft beds they left undisturbed and slept instead on the bare floor. At midnight they arose and prayed aloud. This was kept up throughout Lent, with the result that the ladies were cured of their doubts.

At this time he escorted a certain Bishop to a public disputation, perhaps the only one to take place during this period. The Bishop complied with Dominic's suggestion that they walk to the designated city barefoot and unattended. They lost their way and had to ask direction. The man questioned was an Albigensian who gladly offered to be their guide, secretly intending to play a sore trick on the travelers. He led them over a narrow path, through a stiff undergrowth of brambles which tore their bare feet. When the man noticed that instead of boiling with indignation, Dominic remained calm and intoned a hymn, he admitted his malice, begged forgiveness, and eventually returned to the true faith.

At Carcassonne Dominic confided to a Cistercian monk that God had given him a glimpse into the future. In the Battle of Muret, he said, a king would lose his life. The Cistercian conjectured that this prophecy concerned the Crown Prince of France, who had fled there for safety, but Dominic did not agree. In the battle it was King Peter of Aragon who died. Many other statements of contemporaries refer to this period, all painting a picture of an apostle working quietly and steadily at the conversion of souls while war was raging all around.

MURET

Abbot Arnold of Citeaux probably never bound himself to continue the peaceful attempt of converting the Albigensians. Peter of Castelnau had honestly tried to make Diego's method workable, but changed his mind when the people turned against him. Since then both these legates advocated a military Crusade and tried to bring about an alliance between the French earls and barons for this purpose. Many of these were ready to take up arms, but on the stipulation that Count Raymond of Toulouse do likewise. This condition was not unreasonable, because the Albigensians had their headquarters in his country and this would undoubtedly become the scene of the conflict. Peter therefore tried to win over Count Raymond to their plan. The two met at the famous

Abbey of St. Giles to talk things over. All entreaties, warnings, and promises were powerless to move the Count to collaborate. His conduct is easily understood, because to take up arms would mean fighting against his own subjects and exposing his territory to wrack and ruin. Neither was Raymond free from the suspicion of favoring the heresy. It was at this time that Peter of Castelnau, as Papal Legate, threatened the Count with excommunication, which was followed shortly by the Legate's assassination by one of the Count's squires. This murder excited great horror in Catholic circles. Some thought it was the work of a fanatic; others suspected that the murderer had been hired by Raymond. Innocent, who up to this time had remained peacefully aloof from the events, now felt that his dignity as Pope had been offended in the murder of his legate. Previously the insistence of the two legates, Arnold and Peter, had been powerless to make him launch a crusade for the conversion of the heretics, but now he was convinced that only a crusade would end the evil. The military crusade, a wild and bloody motley of political and religious feuds, may be said to have begun on January 15, 1208, the day of Legate Peter's assassination.

The Pope invited the French King, Philip Augustus, to whose supremacy the Count of Toulouse was subject, to supervise the project. This sovereign, however, declined on the grounds that it would arouse the enmity of England and Germany, but he gave permission for all his vassals and subjects to join the Crusade. Thereupon the leadership was conferred upon Count Simon de Montfort, a fearless knight but not a flawless one. His cheerful personality, his courage and chivalry, inspired the soldiers to heroism on the battlefield. Simon was a religious Crusader, but not a soldier without faults. He lacked prudence and moderation, especially in prosperity. When he set forth with a splendid army in 1209, he rejoiced as if victory were already an established fact. Carcassonne, Fanjeaux, and Beziers were conquered; for the smaller cities and villages resistance was like baying at the moon. Raymond, who was being helped by King Peter of Aragon, traitor to the Catholic cause, placed his hopes in a decisive battle in which the troops of both parties would contend for the victory. This occurred at Muret on September 14, 1213; here again Simon's success was roseate. Raymond escaped death by flight, King Peter fell in battle, and Toulouse with the surrounding country was occupied by the Crusaders.

If Simon had come to peace terms after the victorious Battle of Muret, then the sole purpose of the Crusade, the overthrow of the Albigensians, would have been secured and history would recall his memory as that of the flawless Crusader. But he did not make a peace treaty. He was appointed Viscount of Beziers and after the occupation of Toulouse the entire countryside was under his jurisdiction. It is probable that Simon only intended to exercise this authority long enough to complete the recent military conquest. The son of the defeated Count, named Raymond after his father, had fortified his position in the fortress of Beaucaire. Simon besieged this fortification with the greater part of his troops, leaving behind in Toulouse only a very insufficient garrison. This was the clear sign for the inhabitants of Toulouse, many of whom were out of sympathy with Simon, to signal Raymond to recapture their city. He did so without opposition, thus putting a decisive end to Simon's success in war. The latter once more attempted to recover Toulouse, and was killed in battle on June 26, 1218.

If we explain the continuance of the war after the decisive Battle of Muret from the viewpoint that Simon was only trying to strengthen his position, then his treatment of Albigensian prisoners-of-war is unjustifiable, because he occasioned their wholesale slaughter. Neither can we excuse him on the grounds of a papal order, because Innocent had only authorized him to effect a confiscation of property and deportation of obstinate heretics. To put the blame on one or other Legate in whose counsel Simon trusted does not gloss over his guilt. The fearless Knight's memory is tainted. Simon's oldest son, Amaury, lost everything his father had conquered. Neither did Raymond long enjoy the mastery in Toulouse; in 1229 the district came into the possession of France.

At first sight it may seem strange that an intimate friendship should exist between Simon de

Montfort and Dominic. Their personalities were in sharp contrast; the rough soldier could easily have domineered the gentle apostle. But such was not the case. They represent the two courses approved by the Church for the attainment of the same goal. Dominic tried to convert the Albigensians by preaching and example; Simon pursued the same purpose by military power. Simon knew of Dominic's patient missionary labors among the Albigensians and was determined to maintain the good thus far accomplished. Because of his special protection Prouille remained unscathed, even though for several years surrounded by military maneuvers. By his generous donations, Simon became one of the outstanding benefactors of this first Dominican establishment.

To this partnership of interests was added personal inclination. Simon paid Dominic the esteem which high-minded men of the world instinctively bestow upon those who live up to spiritual ideals. As for Dominic, he would have had to renounce his own knightly ancestry in order not to appreciate the fearless chivalry of the devout Simon. Consequently we frequently find these two men together between the years 1209 and 1218. If a battle occurred in the vicinity of Prouille, Dominic could surely be seen passing among the troops. He had not incited them to take up arms, as Bishop Faulkes had formerly done, nor had he himself put on the helmet and brandished the sword as Deacon William of Paris is said to have done. Dominic's only aim was to reconcile the sinner with God before the battle; during and after the fray he could be seen passing among the soldiers, consoling the wounded and dying. Tradition and history tell us that Dominic was at Muret in a neighboring church, praying the Rosary with arms extended, while De Montfort and his troops took the field. Simon may have counted upon Dominic's nearness in time of battle so that in case of fatal injury his friend would help him at the crossing of the bar. This hope was not realized.

Dominic had a vision in which he beheld a huge tree to whose branches the birds flocked for shelter. The tree suddenly toppled, and all the birds flew away. In this vision he foresaw the death of Simon, the support of the entire Crusade. Whenever Dominic withdrew from the scene of battle, he first bade farewell to Simon and each time circumstances confirmed the apprehension that in his absence the above-mentioned vision was nearing fulfillment. Upon his return from Rome in 1215, and again in 1216, Dominic found his friend still alive. But when he took leave of Simon in the fall of 1217, in order to make a visitation of the Italian foundations and settle business affairs with the Roman curia, the parting in the camp outside Toulouse was depressing, because the fighting forces were considerably diminished, there were forebodings of the city's conquest, and Dominic's absence would very probably be lengthy. As a matter of fact, Simon was killed in battle while Dominic was in Bologna assisting the hard-pressed community by his counsels and transactions. Simon had been dead a long time when Dominic again saw Prouille and Toulouse. The General Chapter of the Dominican Order in 1256 ordained that in the Martyrology for June 26 the following encomium should be read: "On this day is commemorated the death in Toulouse of Lord Simon, Count of Montfort, zealous lover of the faith, the intimate friend of St. Dominic." The purpose of this yearly announcement is to remind the brethren to pray for him and his entire family, whose history is so closely linked to the Order.

The chronicles of the Dominican Order relate that two of Simon's daughters became Dominican nuns. We are not told the name of the first. The second, named Amica, wife of Seigneur de Joigny, is described as a devout and illustrious woman. Her great desire was that her only son, John de Montfort, would become a Dominican. This wish was realized when in 1245 the young man joined the Crusade of St. Louis to the Holy Land. Falling sick at Cypress he remembered his mother's prayers, begged to be clothed in the Dominican habit, and so died as a member of the Order. Amica's one real grief was that as a woman she could not become a Preacher. She founded the Monastery of Dominican Nuns in Montargis where she herself took the veil and died a holy death.

TOULOUSE

An apostolic idea was expanding in Dominic's mind between 1207 and 1215, the very years when the hell hound of war was threatening to slay the missionary project. Instead of confining himself and his companions to southern France, he intended to spread the good work to the four quarters of the globe. After much reflection, Dominic stated that the aim of the work was to preach the Gospel to all nations, as Christ had commanded. This missionary field was to be absolutely boundless; it was to include heretics and Moors, believers and unbelievers, faithful Catholics and backsliders. In order to appreciate the boldness of this adventure we must recall the condition of the Church in the thirteenth century. The life of the majority of the clergy, and even of many bishops, was a scandal to the laity. Many priests were outstanding in ignorance, engrossed in the feverish hunt for benefices, and negligent in preaching the Word of God. This neglect of preaching was, perhaps, their most obvious omission, so that many a parish was without a pastor at all, and the pulpit nothing more than an empty piece of furniture.

Preaching has always been considered the prerogative of bishops, but in large dioceses it is impossible for even the most zealous bishop to preach personally the Word of God to all the people. This is where the local clergy fit into the picture. As they represent the bishop in the celebration of Holy Mass and the administration of the sacraments, so they should also preach in his stead. That is the ideal, but the actual condition of thirteenth-century priesthood left much to be desired. Although the Church had tried to rid herself of these evils, and within sixty years convoked three general councils for this purpose, the first effective movement of reform came from the laity. It seemed as if the laxity of the clergy awakened the people to a consciousness of their own lack of religion. Here and there groups of men, under the leadership of Peter Waldes, began to expound the faith, but the bishops objected on the principle that it was an encroachment on their episcopal office. At first Pope Alexander III authorized the preaching of the Waldensians, as the followers of Waldes were called. But it soon became evident that these laymen, without theological training, were in danger of inaccuracy and unorthodoxy in matters of faith. Waldes went to Rome about the matter. The Pope commended his zeal but ordered him not to preach in future without permission of the local bishop. Waldes did not long obey this injunction and explained his course of action with the assertion that the power to preach did not depend on the sacrament of Holy Orders nor on the sanction of the bishop, but on the individual's vocation which consisted in imitating the Apostles in the observance of perfect poverty. From then on the Church had to regard Waldes as a heretic.

Dominic knew that public preaching is not the duty of the laity. He accepted only priests as active assistants in his missionary labors. When formulating his project for preaching the Gospel to all peoples he did not try to obtain from Rome a blanket approval for his followers to exercise their preaching apostolate independently of the local bishops. On the contrary, they were to be subject to the bishop and preach in a diocese only with his permission. This staved off the complaints which had been raised against the heretical preachers.

Neither did Dominic agree with Waldes' opinion that the apostolic life, especially the practice of absolute poverty, automatically licensed an individual to preach the Gospel; however, he did admit that a preacher without property has a better chance of success than one whose wealth might arouse men's greed. He remembered Christ's words to His Apostles before sending them to announce the joyful tidings: "Do not possess gold, nor silver, nor money in your purses. Nor scrip for your journey, nor two coats, nor shoes, nor a staff; for the workman is worthy of his meat" (Mt. 10:9-11). But he also knew the Church's infallible decision that some of Christ's words are to be considered as counsels, not as commands. For twelve centuries these particular words of the Master had been regarded as a counsel and had helped many to arrive at religious perfection. The hermits lived in poverty, but they earned a livelihood by their manual labor. The monks renounced all right of private ownership, but the monastery could own property to provide for the needs of the community. Dominic had himself taken the vow of poverty as an Augustinian canon and had practiced absolute poverty ever since the meeting with the despondent Cistercians at Montpellier. In developing his plans for the establishment of an Order to be totally dedicated to preaching the Gospel, he injected perfect poverty into the project because he was convinced that the people would not be converted by missionaries whom the Church had enriched with benefices.

In 1215 Peter Seila, a wealthy merchant, gave Dominic a house in Toulouse and later joined him as preacher. Other disciples were quick to follow. With Toulouse as their headquarters, Dominic and these companions began a wandering existence. Before long the house at Toulouse proved inadequate as a combination recruiting station for missionaries and a convalescent home for the sick brethren. Bishop Faulke, who rejoiced that his diocese was the headquarters of such an excellent project, bequeathed in 1215 "to Brother Dominic and his companions, vowed to travel about barefoot, preaching the Gospel in evangelical poverty," and whom he, Faulke, had appointed as preachers of his bishopric, a sixth part of the tithes designated for the cathedral so that these preachers who had voluntarily embraced poverty for Christ's sake might not be deprived of necessities in time of sickness and rest. By this donation the Preaching Brethren received external security. Dominic tried to form his companions interiorly according to the Rule he had designed for them. This Rule was quite a novelty at that time and the followers of the ancient monastic Rules very likely perked their ears in mistrust. In this Rule Dominic designated work for the salvation of souls through preaching as the Order's aim, and absolute poverty as one of the chief means to attain this end. The next step was to obtain papal approbation. Thereafter Dominic would cease to be a Canon Regular of St. Augustine.

Here we may ask whether Dominic experienced an interior struggle in making this transition from the time-honored Augustinian Order to a new-fledged preaching institute. We must remember that Canon Law permits a religious to join a stricter Order with his Superior's consent. The projected Order of Preachers certainly offered a higher form of religious life than that of the Augustinian Canons. From the standpoint of legitimacy, Dominic's design presented no obstacle. Nevertheless, it has always been thought that he did not make this change without an interior struggle, because such an action always bears the appearance of infidelity to one's first community. To renounce the dignity of being a Canon of Osma caused him no heart twinge, but very likely the breaking of pledged loyalty with the Augustinian Order stirred up some rough weather within him. The Church's dire need for worthy and zealous preachers made him willing to leave the Augustinian Order and take upon himself the appearance of divided allegiance.

IV

THE FOUNDATION OF THE ORDER OF PREACHERS

THE DECREE OF THE LATERAN COUNCIL

DURING the years in which Dominic developed the plan by which the Albigensian mission project was changed into a world-wide venture, and sketched the outlines of an Order dedicated to announce the Gospel to all peoples, he received various miraculous signs of God's approval. His zeal for the faith received divine approbation in the miracle of the fire trial at Fanjeaux. The heretics requested the fire trial with the stipulation: "Let us throw your book into the fire. If it burns, then our doctrine is the truth. If it remains unhurt, then truth is on the side of its writer, Dominic." The book did not merely remain uninjured, but rose majestically above the flames. The heretics tried to hush up this miracle, but it was made known by a soldier who had witnessed it.

Dominic considered sacred study as the fuel to be constantly thrown into the fire of preaching. He always carried with him on his preaching expeditions the Gospel of St. Matthew and the Epistles of St. Paul, and read them whenever not prevented by other duties. On one occasion, as he was wading across a stream and had tucked up his habit, the books fell into the water and were carried away by the current. He confided his grief at this loss to a pious woman who gave him a night's lodging. The next day a fisherman brought the books to the kind hostess. He had found them on the riverbank, in good condition, although not protected by any waterproof covering. Thereafter they were doubly precious to Dominic, who regarded this restoration a sign of God's approval of his love of sacred scripture.

In 1211 Dominic's apostolic wanderings brought him close to the river Garonne, not far from Toulouse. While he was there, a group of English pilgrims bound for St. James in Compostela tried to cross the river in a small boat. The vessel capsized and all were in danger of drowning. Someone called for Dominic, who was praying in the Church of St. Anthony near the scene of the accident. He came, made the Sign of the Cross over the waters, and all were saved. This was taken as a confirmation of his life of prayer.

Another time Dominic himself had used the ferry. At the end of the crossing the ferryman asked the usual fare, but Dominic told him he had no money. This stirred up the man's anger, so he grabbed Dominic's cloak and demanded angrily: "Either the money or this cloak!" Dominic looked toward heaven, then pointing to the ground said to the man: "Permit me to go ahead, and take for payment what is lying here." The required money was on the ground. Herein he could see heaven's stamp of approval on his ideal of absolute poverty.

Bishop Faulke had approved the preaching

project: if the project was confined to the diocese of Toulouse, this approval would suffice. But Dominic looked beyond the plains of Toulouse and saw the crying need for worthy announcement of the gospel truths. The examination and approval of a new religious order is a papal concern. In 1215 Dominic could count only six companions. It is doubtful that he expected to obtain papal approbation for an undertaking which numbered so few members, but because at that time a favorable occasion presented itself, Dominic made the attempt. Pope Innocent III had convoked a General Council in Rome on November 1, 1215. This Lateran Council was to deliberate on the errors of contemporary heresies, the Albigensians, the Waldensians, the Lombard poor men, on the duty of bishops to provide worthy and sufficient explanation of the Word of God, the reform of relaxed monasteries, and the retaking of the Holy Land. Bishop Faulke decided to attend and took Dominic with him as canon-theologian. They reached the Eternal City by the end of September, 1215. Dominic hoped to obtain papal protection for Prouille so that in spite of the unsettled political situation, his religious establishment would remain in peaceful possession of property. He also planned to reap the benefit of the occasion and have his preaching project sanctioned as a religious order. The first petition was readily granted on October 8, 1215, but the idea of a world-wide religious order, grouped under one head, was too bold and novel for immediate approval. Pope Innocent praised what had been accomplished thus far, but did not grant the supreme approbation. To entrust a select man with the teaching of sacred doctrine in a particular country for a definite period is one thing, but to approve a group of men to teach everywhere and forever is quite another matter. Pope Innocent would not take such a leap into the dark.

The old chronicles record two incidents which took place while the Order was hanging in the balance. While praying at the tomb of the Apostles Peter and Paul, Dominic had a vision of the Saviour, provoked by the corruption of Christendom, ready to send down lightning flashes of chastisement. The Virgin Mother approached her Son and introduced Him to two men, telling Him they would transform the world. Dominic recognized one of them as himself, the other he could not identify. The following day he met Francis of Assisi and recognized him as the companion of his vision. He embraced Francis and exclaimed: "Let us remain together and be partners!" This did not imply a union of the two Orders because the two Founders had entirely different ideals and their spiritual families have always remained distinct, but it shows the parallel destinies of the two Orders. Dominicans heal mankind's diseases of the mind; Franciscans, the diseases of the heart. To the Holy Father, wavering between duty and doubt, God made known His will in a vision of the Lateran Basilica, where the Council was convening. The Basilica was on the verge of collapse, but the priest Dominic approached and held up the tottering walls. Innocent did not want to contravene the Council's recent legislation that no more religious Rules should be introduced, but that the already existing ones be better observed. Convinced that this vision was God's way of instructing him, he advised Dominic to return to Toulouse and confer with his companions about adopting an already existing Rule and developing their constitutions on this framework. When the choice was settled, then he would approve the Order. Some writers have stated that Dominic left Rome with a heavy heart because his original plan for the Preaching Order had not been sanctioned. However, it seems more probable that he was lighthearted at this turn of events, already determined to pattern the new Constitutions on the Augustinian Rule under which he had lived so many years, and so remain loyal to his first profession.

THE RULE OF ST. AUGUSTINE

Bishop Faulke and Dominic returned to Toulouse determined to put into practice the canons of the recent Council convoked by Innocent III, canons which reveal how very much alive both Pope and Council were to the manifold evils that plagued all Christendom. The Council's confirmation of Count Simon de Montfort's possession of Toulouse was gratifying to Faulke because there had been friction between him and the two-faced Raymond, whereas union existed between him and the single-minded Simon. Dominic was also happy because he had obtained papal protection for Prouille, and the semi-approval for the Preaching Order. Faulkes had no doubts as to which Rule would be chosen; he realized that it would not be the Cistercian Rule, which he himself had observed before his episcopal elevation, because like all the old monastic rules it underscored separation from the world and personal sanctification, making the apostolate for souls consist chiefly in example, prayer, and penance. He knew that was a worthy ideal, but that it was not the only standard of spiritual perfection. The Church herself is closely allied to another criterion; she ordains priests to strive for the salvation of their fellow men. This does not exclude the obligation of self-sanctification, but, according to St. Paul, requires a rigid application to the task: "I crucify my body and bring it into subjection, lest having preached to others, I myself should become a castaway" (1 Cor. 9:27). This was the ideal in St. Augustine's mind as he composed his Rule, which may be described as a priest's interpretation of how priests should observe Christ's gospel counsels, beginning with the fundamental command, "Let God be loved above all things and the neighbor for God's sake." No particular observances are marked out except the sharing of goods in common, prayer, frugality, vigilance, and fraternal correction of faults.

Dominic had made profession according to the Augustinian Rule at Osma and had always retained the title, "Canon of Osma." If the Pope had approved Dominic's original Rule, this would have cut him off from the Augustinian family. When this approbation was withheld, he decided to direct the attention of his companions to the Rule of St. Augustine. Thereby he avoided the danger of excessive meddling in the internal government of the Order by the local bishops, something they might have done if the original Rule had been accepted. Since the Augustinian Rule has papal approbation, no bishop can make changes according to personal taste. The adoption of the Augustinian Rule also made it possible for Dominic to draw up a set of Constitutions which would delineate the distinct purpose of the Order — the salvation of souls through preaching and teaching — and determine very exactly the means to attain this end. Such separate Constitutions were adopted by every monastery observing the Augustinian Rule. In the Cathedral Chapter of Osma, these Constitutions dealt only with the pastoral duties of the parish. The Premonstratensians served several mission churches from the parish church where a number of priests lived a community life, an arrangement which gave the individual priests a double advantage. In the first place, they were not bound to one particular church; in the second place, members could be shifted from one monastery to another, thus establishing a constantly moving army of preachers prepared to go wherever necessity called. Instead of hindering Dominic's project, the enforced delay advanced it.

What appeared as a stumbling block was in reality a stepping stone.

The Augustinian Rule lays great emphasis on the choral chant of the Divine Office. In spite of the possibility that this might take away too much time from study and preaching, Dominic chose to retain the choral chant. The directive inserted in the Constitutions, that the chant should keep moving at a good pace, may very probably have been the Founder's own suggestion.

According to thirteenth century standards, the choral celebration of the Divine Office was an essential element of an Order of priests. Prayer is the obligation not only of an individual but of every community, especially of a religious organization. Dominic was organizing a community of priests who were already bound to the recitation of the breviary; so it followed as a natural consequence that this private prayer must become its corporate prayer. Dominic was influenced in this decision by his spirit of faith, which told him that this official prayer of the Church is the surest means of drawing God's blessings upon the preaching of his followers. While chanting the breviary in choir they would be united with the entire praying Church. He also knew from experience that the meaning of the sacred writings envelops the suppliant more completely during public prayer than in private recitation. This offered an immediate advantage for the Order's particular purpose. Study has a tendency to dry up the emotional side of human nature and make a man insensible to the needs of others, whereas the Divine Office said chorally tends to make him an apostle and share with others what he has acquired in prayer and study.

The early historians of the Order tell us that Dominic's devotion at the Divine Office rivaled that of any monk or canon. This was not only true during the quiet years at Osma, but also during his journeys and missionary labors when he recited the Office in common with Diego and the other clerics. After the establishment of the Order, the Founder's zeal for the celebration of the Divine Office shone forth more brightly than ever. He was never absent from any Hour and could even be seen kneeling in choir before time, setting his soul in order for the sacred duty soon to begin. During the Office he was all fervor, and his resonant voice was the veritable pillar upholding the chant. When he noticed weariness overcoming the Brethren he would make his way among them, and by a few words or gestures reanimate their zeal in singing God's praises.

Love for the great saint of Hippo was another deciding factor in the choice of the Augustinian Rule. This man with the glowing heart, the brilliant mind, the eloquent tongue, and the persuasive pen had been his personal ideal. Augustine should, Dominic maintained, also be "the observed of all observers" in the entire Order. Dominic's first concern when arriving at Toulouse in the spring of 1216 was to assemble his companions, who had increased from six to sixteen during his absence, and tell them of the Pope's kindly reception and his promise to confirm the Order after they had chosen a Rule. Perhaps he first explained to them that the Rule of St. Benedict was too unwieldy for their purpose, and then proceeded to point out the elasticity of the Augustinian Rule and of the Constitutions which would apply this Rule to their particular needs. The Brethren understood their Founder's wishes and made choice of St. Augustine's Rule.

THE CONSTITUTIONS OF THE ORDER OF PREACHERS

The Rule having been chosen, the next step was to draw up the Constitutions, a practical supplement which would suit an Order whose purposes were the attainment of individual perfection through prayer and study, and the salvation of souls by teaching and preaching. St. Augustine's Rule begins with these words: "Before all things, dear brethren, let us love God, and after Him our neighbor." What follows is a summons to observe the two great commandments of God-love and neighbor-love by faithful observance of the ten commandments and by voluntarily embracing the three gospel counsels of spontaneous poverty, perpetual chastity, and willing obedience. Because this practical charity was already practiced by the Canons Regular within their parish limits, and by the Premonstratensians in the wider area of the monastery's precincts, the proposed plan of the new Order to extend its preaching to the whole world, without attaching the individual preacher to a particular house, but maintaining him in complete subordination to a central authority, was only taking a step forward in the natural process of development. It was walking in the footsteps of Augustine, who, although Bishop of Hippo, instructed all Africa and the entire Christian world throughout the centuries by his preaching and writing.

An unprecedented feature of the Constitutions was the emphasis on intellectual labors. With the older monks and canons, the greater part of the day was devoted to prayer and manual work, but the very purpose of the Preaching Order necessitated an intense application to study as a preparation for preaching. To provide an atmosphere conducive to study, silence was to be rigorously observed throughout the monastery. We have seen in the account of Dominic's missionary labors in southern France that he argued with the Albigensian heretics and confounded their theories by a theological defense of Catholic belief. His purpose in gathering disciples around him was precisely to defeat science by science; and the popular but careful, clear exposition of the deepest mysteries of faith, which is the essential foundation of all sound morality, was to be the message of his Order's preachings. For this purpose he sought out, for the adequate training of his first disciples, the most renowned masters in theology and philosophy. As soon as they were established in Peter Seila's house in Toulouse, he took his little band of six to Master Alexander Stavensby, one of the best minds of those times. The interesting account of this meeting is related by Blessed Humbert. While preparing his lectures early one morning, the illustrious theologian, Master Stavensby, fell into a slumber. He saw in a prophetic vision the whole heretical country submerged in the darkness of night. But behold, in the horizon seven stars were rising, climbing rapidly in the sky, growing in brightness and multiplying themselves so prodigiously that they illumined all the earth. On awakening and noting that it was already broad daylight, Master Stavensby immediately proceeded to school. As he entered, Dominic and his six companions presented themselves. They were preachers, they said, who were evangelizing the region of Toulouse and were desirous to hear the lessons of the Master. Master Stavensby, perceiving then the symbolic meaning of the seven stars, received them as sent from heaven. In later years the spread of the Preaching Order over the whole world and the remarkable conversions accompanying the preaching of the brethren allowed no room for doubt in Alexander's mind that Dominic and his six companions were signified by the seven stars, and he took pleasure in designating himself as first teacher of the new Order.

Another unprecedented feature of the Constitutions was the principle that dispensation from Rule, under obedience, is as sacred as the Rule itself. This meant that each superior in his own monastery could relieve the brethren from fasts, abstinences, and prayer in common so that they could devote more time and energy to study, preaching, and the good of souls. This was Dominic's way of saying that the Rule and Constitutions must not come between a Dominican and his work for souls. Thus a religious may be dispensed from certain tasks while engaged in intellectual or apostolic assignments, and this not as a peace offering to man's weakness but a dispensation made to allow him to do more for God. Herein we can also see the trust Dominic placed in his followers, for the right to ask and give dispensations puts both subjects and superiors on their honor not to use this pliant power more than is really necessary.

Another innovation which shows the trust Dominic placed in his companions was the stipulation that the Rule and Constitutions do not bind under sin. When some of the brethren called this principle into question by saying that more exact observance would result if violations were made sinful, Dominic was so moved that he declared he would go to every monastery and destroy the Constitutions with his own knife rather than bind men with such a heavy iron chain. He was legislating for intellectual beings, not for human machines; therefore faults against the Rule and Constitutions are not sinful unless they are committed through contempt or if the superior has given a formal precept, which is rarely done.

Blessed Humbert stated the spirit of the Dominican Constitutions in a nutshell when he said that Dominic took from the Premonstratensian Constitutions whatever he found in them that was "difficult, beautiful, or wise." In these words he is paying tribute to Dominic's spirit of chivalry, which would not let him rest content with what was easy or comfortable, but deemed the beautiful inseparable from the arduous and wise, for there was nothing fanatical in the Constitutions.

PAPAL APPROBATION

Dominic and his companions had set up a private oratory in the house which Peter Seila had given them, but this did not fulfill the Augustinian requirement of a public church wherein the Divine Office is offered in the name of all the faithful. It was Bishop Faulke who helped them out of, this deadlock by giving the Church of St. Romanus in Toulouse to the young community. Although it was not in a very good condition, it would answer the purpose. The transfer took place in July, 1216. Now that everything was arranged according to the Augustinian Rule and Pope Innocent's instructions, Dominic set out once more for Rome in September, 1216. A disconcerting surprise awaited him there. On July 16 Innocent III had died, the greatest of medieval popes, whose life had apparently been so essential to the Church in this troubled period. Dominic may well have added, "He was also necessary for me and my project." Innocent had shown himself favorable to the plan of an Order dedicated to the task of preaching divine truth and had promised to give it papal approval as soon as it had been firmly grounded on a previously ratified Rule. The condition was fulfilled, but Pope Innocent was dead. Dominic no doubt wondered whether the next Pope would carry out his predecessor's promise. Popes are also human, and the new incumbent does not always agree with his predecessor in matters which do not involve faith or morals.

When Dominic reached Rome in October, 1216, he learned that Cardinal Cencio Savelli had been elected pope on the preceding July 18, taking the name of Honorius III. As Supreme Pontiff he was bound to execute the decrees of the Lateran Council, but the approval of a new religious Order was an open question. Honorius, who had known about the Preaching Order since the days of the Lateran Council, received the Founder cordially and listened willingly to his petition for papal approval of an Order which offered to the Church the very men designated by Canon 10 of the recent Council: "Because it often happens that the Bishops cannot personally preach the Word of God to the people, we command that they appoint certain men for the apostolate of preaching, men mighty in word and deed." Pope Honorius assured Dominic in his first audience that he intended to carry out his predecessor's promise regarding the Order of Preachers, but Dominic waited three months while the Constitutions were being sifted by cardinals and theologians. The official approbation, given December 22, 1216, was set forth in a twofold form. In the first Bull, Pope Honorius III declares to "Brother Dominic, Prior of St. Romanus in Toulouse, and his brethren who have or will embrace the religious life," that he approves the Order and takes it under his special protection because "the brethren of the Order will become champions of the faith and true lights of the world."

In a second Bull issued on the same day, the Order was officially recognized as an Order of Canons Regular observing the Rule of St. Augustine. The titles are then set forth; and the Church of St. Romanus, Prouille, the revenues transmitted to the brethren by Bishop Faulke, all are gathered together under the Pope's safekeeping. Next follow a number of privileges customarily conferred on every Augustinian Chapter. This Bull, composed in a very solemn manner and signed by eighteen cardinals, remained for many years the weightiest document in Dominican history. Dr. Scheeben has shown that the first Bull, even though its form is less grandiose, excels the second in importance because by it. the Order of Preachers is elevated from the usual category of Augustinian Chapters among which the second classifies it. Within the Augustinian family and under papal direction, a unique organization had been established, the first religious Order in the modern sense of the word. To the many Augustinian and

Benedictine houses, the Holy See had given separate confirmation for the establishment of each individual convent, whereas a religious Order is a collection of monasteries grouped together not only under obedience to the same Rule but also under the authority of a single supreme head. Dominic had asked and obtained the confirmation, not only of the house of St. Romanus, but of the entire Order of which it was the headquarters.

After the Easter of 1217 Dominic set out again for Toulouse; and his journey must have been a joyful one now that the Order was confirmed by Christ's Vicar as a world-wide apostolate of truth. The cornerstone had been solidly laid, and Dominic was confident that in time the spiritual structure would be completed. There was no time to waste because the brethren in Toulouse needed his presence.

V

THE DISPERSION OF THE BRETHREN

PROUILLE AS MONASTERY OF THE SECOND ORDER

DURING Dominic's long absence the brethren at Toulouse had become heavy-hearted, a state not difficult to understand. Simon de Montfort having gathered his troops at Beaucaire in order to conquer that city, Toulouse was consequently left practically without a garrison and on September 1, 1217, Count Raymond re-entered the city. All this boded ill for the Crusaders. The brethren must have asked themselves what would become of the monastery, and even of the entire nascent Order, when their greatest benefactor, Simon de Montfort, would no longer be able to protect them. They also knew that Bishop Faulke was weary of episcopal responsibilities and had petitioned Rome to accept his resignation. But the most distressing source of worry to the brethren was their Father's long absence and the fact that no information had reached them concerning the approbation of the Order. Several of them became so discouraged that they considered quitting Toulouse and even discussed what Order they would join. When in December word reached him at Rome about the activity of the blue devils at Toulouse, Dominic sent the brethren tidings as soon as he could of the Order's approval, and he requested the Pope to address a special letter to them. Possessing this letter, dated January 21,1217, and the two approbative Bulls, Dominic set out on his homeward journey. Pope Honorius' advice to Bishop Faulke, that now was not the time to look for rest but to bend his back to the burden, also applied perfectly to the brethren. When Dominic reached Toulouse, the crestfallen soon began to see the sun which had been hiding behind the clouds and all were again what they had been previously, his true-blue companions, eager to share in his labors and hardships. The thought of leaving Toulouse, which some of them had entertained, was now to be quickly realized, although through an entirely different motive from that of despondency.

Dominic immediately set to work drilling his sixteen companions in faithful observance of the Rule and Constitutions, teaching them the particular spirit of the new Order, and animating them with great zeal for the work of saving souls through preaching. If any of them fancied that he would now establish a model monastery at St. Romanus, there gather more disciples, and methodically accomplish every minute direction, their reverie would not last long. Humanly speaking, this would have been the best thing to do; but only a few months after the Order's formal establishment and his return to Toulouse, Dominic announced that he did not intend to hoard up the grain, but to sow it broadcast. His friends objected. Some of the brethren boggled, but Dominic, who in other matters acquiesced so readily to the suggestions and opinions of others, was adamant in this intention. He was determined to disperse his followers throughout the world; he even hinted that he would leave Toulouse himself. His reasons for this course of action were questioned at that time, and are being probed even to this day. The fresh triumph of Albigensianism has been adduced by some; but Dominic, who had persevered for over ten years under the selfsame circumstances, would not scatter his disciples because of political unrest. Others have cited the Church's dire need of apostles to preach the faith, but by itself this would not explain his procedure, because seventeen preachers would have been unequal to the task. In recent years it has been said that the Founder was influenced by the great confidence he had in his project. Although Dominic was optimistic about the Order's stability, a higher motive was necessary to embolden him to make such a flip of the coin. To all objections against the proposed dispersion, Dominic replied: "Let me do as I plan. I know what I am about. Hoarded, the grain rots; cast to the winds, it brings forth fruit." Dominic's immediate successor as Master General of the Order, Blessed Jordan, tells us that Dominic decided on this dispersion because of a vision of the Princes of the Apostles which had been granted him during the long period of waiting in Rome. Peter gave him a

staff, Paul offered him a book. If the vision had
ended there, Dominic could hardly have seen in it
a reason to scatter his brethren. But after hearing
in the vision the Apostles' command, "Go and
preach!" he saw his companions spread themselves
over the world two by two, equipped with staff and
book. The memory of this vision was the goad
which gave him no rest until the seed had been
sown.

August 15, 1217, was the day set for casting
the sixteen companions to the four winds. Dominic
celebrated the Mass of Mary's Assumption at
Prouille, surrounded by his companions and the
Sisters. After Mass all made solemn vows into the
hands of their spiritual father, because previous to
this there had been no other bond than their own
constancy. Then the thunderbolt struck: "Go and
preach. Go on foot, without money, without worry
about tomorrow, begging your bread." A group of
four was sent to Spain: Peter of Madrid, Michael of
Uzero, Dominic of Segovia, and Suero of Gomez. To
Paris were sent Mannes, Michael of Fabra, Bertrand
of Garrigua, Lawrence of England, John of Navarre,
Oderic the Norman lay brother, and Matthew of
France. Peter Seila and Thomas remained at
Toulouse, and Noel and William Claret at Prouille.
If Bishop Faulke or Simon de Montfort had hoped
against hope that Dominic himself would at least
stay at Prouille or Toulouse to keep watch and
ward, they were soon disappointed because he was
determined to share personally in the Order's
world-wide unfurling by visiting the houses the

brethren would establish, but keeping Rome as his headquarters. Stephen of Metz was to be his first traveling companion.

Peter and Thomas were appointed to carry on the work at Toulouse. In 1218 Peter came to Paris; perhaps war conditions made it perilous for him to remain at Toulouse, or possibly another had been assigned to replace him. Dominic then sent him to establish the Order at Limoges, where conditions for a foundation were favorable. But Peter, who was by temperament timid and diffident, hesitated because of lack of books and scholastic training. Dominic brushed aside these arguments, saying: "Go, my son! Have confidence in God. I will remember your needs twice daily in prayer. Do not fail me, for you will win many souls." The Founder's optimism stirred up Peter's spirit and the prophecy came true.

Prouille was also provided for. From this we see clearly that the dispersion of the brethren did not imply the abandonment of previous fields of labor. Dominic was really obliged to care for Prouille because of the conditions under which Pope Honorius had supported the preaching project. If the original Constitutions had been approved, then the new Order of Preaching Brethren would have had no legal association with Prouille, which had been recognized as an Augustinian Monastery in October, 1216. Although Dominic very likely would have continued providing for this monastery of nuns, the Order would not have been under obligation to look after its concerns. Every succeeding Master General would have been free to recall the brethren from Prouille and refer the nuns to the Augustinian Canons: but in establishing his Order on the Augustinian Rule and linking his spiritual family to that of St. Augustine, Dominic accepted the responsibility of providing for the temporal and spiritual needs of the Sisters. We can prove this from the fact that the brethren whom he appointed to Prouille were in charge of its external administration and served as chaplains, confessors, and spiritual directors to the community. In ordinary parlance the nuns of Prouille are usually called the Dominican Second Order, whereas the Preaching Brethren are termed the First Order. In reality both divisions were founded simultaneously, and the Second Order received papal approbation before the First Order. It seems that Dominic was intent on fastening very securely the bonds between the nuns of Prouille and his Order. As the Brethren were distinct from the Augustinian Canons, so the nuns should also be different from other Augustinian sisterhoods. He gave the same ideal of saving souls by preaching as life's purpose to these cloistered nuns as to his preaching sons, who had the world for their cell and the hills and mountains as monastic walls. Dominic would have been glad if the Sisters were not bound too strictly by the law of enclosure so that they could more readily exercise all the corporal and spiritual works of mercy; but now that walls and grilles separated them from the laity, the care of the sick and down-

and-out had to be greatly restricted. The only external works that remained were the education of girls and instruction of heretics desirous of returning to the Church, and the dispensing of alms at the monastery gate. The Sisters would zealously devote themselves to these activities, not fixing their intention on the alleviation of material distress but on the salvation of souls. The practice of corporal mercy should be an occasion of preaching a practical sermon on faith. Besides these direct ministrations the nuns were to assist indirectly at the conversion of mankind by occupying themselves in church sewing, doing laundry, and other relevant works so that the Brethren would have more time to devote to study and preaching.

Nor was Dominic unmindful of the efficacy hidden in the Sisters' life of prayer, penance, and expiation. At Prouille the Divine Office was not executed quickly; on the contrary, he expected the Sisters to celebrate it with solemnity because they were not overburdened with other occupations. Dominic repeatedly exhorted them to pray with heart and soul for the missionary labors of the brethren and his own enterprises. Day in and day out people came to the monastery asking the Sisters to pray for their intentions. A lay sister distributed the material alms at the monastery gate, but a choir nun listened at the parlor grille to the sad tales of those seeking relief from the thousand ills that afflict humanity. This duty required a prudent, experienced religious, skilled in the art of giving counsel and comfort, and knowing what to keep secret and what to disclose to the Sisters in order to incite them to more earnest prayer. Simple people came with their difficulties, with personal or family troubles; princes came with affairs of state; bishops and legates came asking the help of the Sisters' prayers for the needs of individual dioceses and of all Christendom.

The monastery at Prouille was close to Dominic's heart. He nourished its interior development, at first verbally, then by means of the Augustinian Rule, and lastly through the written Constitutions. But it is not the only monastery in southern France dating to the early years of the Order.

In Toulouse Dominic formed a group of women converted from sin into a penitential religious community. This monastery is also mentioned in the Bull of Approval. Another project dear to Dominic was the establishment of an active religious sisterhood, unshackled by walls and grilles; but in this he was too far in advance of his century. What the Sisters of the Third Order Regular are accomplishing today in the realm of Christian charity was already earnestly desired by Dominic at the beginning of the Prouille foundation. The Sisters proved loyal to their Founder even when William Claret, Dominic's first auxiliary at Prouille, entered the Cistercian Order and tried to persuade them to follow his example.

The union established with Prouille also enabled Dominic to carry out his plan of perfect poverty for the Preaching Brethren. The Bull of Approval had designated the possessions of Prouille and the penitential monastery in Toulouse as belonging to the Order, thereby placing the Order of Preachers, in respect to poverty, on the same level as the Augustinian Canons. In his great desire to imitate perfectly the poverty of the homeless Christ and to work more efficaciously for the salvation of souls, Dominic wanted the Brethren to own no real estate. He therefore transferred all possessions to the Sisters. All that remained to the Brethren was their Convent and the ground it occupied. He would also have been happy to renounce all revenues; but because of the uncertainty attending the development of the Order in various countries, he temporarily retained the tithes granted to him by Bishop Faulke. These, however, he considered as alms to be used only according to their original purpose, the care of the sick and convalescent members, and to tide over a new foundation in its first hardships.

MADRID AND SEGOVIA

It is surely a high compliment to Dominic's influence over his companions that not one of them disappointed him when the departure day came. The human heart being so formed that it spontaneously answers trust with trust, they felt honored by the confidence which he had in them, and resolved to measure up to his expectations. Spain, France, and Italy were the missionary goals set before them. Elaborate preparations were unnecessary because these new Apostles were to travel according to the Master's instructions to His disciples, on foot, unencumbered by baggage, begging their daily bread.

This first dispatch shows us a very likable side of Dominic's character, his patriotism. Spain was his homeland; he had not forgotten it during his fourteen-year absence, and he wanted to dispense the Order's first blessings on his countrymen. For this mission he appointed Brother Dominic of Segovia, also called the Spaniard, Michael of Uzero, Peter of Madrid, and Suero Gomez. All four were Spanish by birth and very probably had come to France in response to Diego's plea for assistance in combating the Albigensians. Dominic of Segovia, the leader of the group, was, according to Blessed Jordan's testimony, "a man of great humility, of scant knowledge, but magnificent in virtue."

While Peter and Suero went to Madrid and founded a Convent there, Dominic and Michael went to Segovia. But the well-meaning Dominic had to admit that a prophet is not welcome in his own city. In 1218 they returned discomfited to the Founder, who was then in Rome. After listening to the recital of their wild-goose chase he very probably realized that he had expected too much from these two men. They were not sent back to Spain, but to Bologna to assist the elderly Richard in the foundation he had established there.

Dominic did not give up the idea of

establishing the Order in Spain just because these two disciples had fallen short. Peter and Suero had remained; they did not consider the project beyond the bounds of possibility, so Dominic decided to go to Spain himself. He arrived at Barcelona in 1218, and after fourteen years' absence walked again on his native soil. As a Spaniard this country was dear to him, especially Castile, his boyhood home. It was not for a vacation that he came, but as the black and white hound of his mother's dream, setting the world ablaze with the torch of holy preaching. He visited Calaroga, Gumiel de Izan, Silos, and Osma. Perhaps the old folks who remembered the ardent young canon expressed surprise at this prematurely aged, travel-worn apostle, whose spirit was still on fire. He did not stay here long, but pushed on to join Peter and Suero. Blessed Jordan tells us that Dominic founded two monasteries in Spain, one in Madrid, the other in Segovia. Peter had directed his steps to Madrid because it was his birthplace. With the help of Suero he had interested some young men in the Order and acquired a small house, so the founder had only to key up the interest of the citizens and look around for a more suitable monastery. Enthusiastic young men offered to join the Order, and some young ladies begged him to lead them on the way of perfection. These latter he could not unite in a religious community because the house was hardly large enough for the brethren, but he consoled them with the promise to send them his brother Mannes, who would provide for their spiritual needs. In time the foundation in

Madrid developed into a monastery for nuns after the pattern of Prouille, through the efforts of Mannes.

At Segovia, where Dominic the Spaniard and Michael of Uzero had missed the mark, the Founder promptly established a monastery for men. At the beginning of his stay in that city he lodged with a devout lady. Gerard de Frachet relates an episode which happened at this time and which gives us a good insight to the Founder's penitential spirit. Until then Dominic had worn a coarse shirt, which served as an excellent instrument of penance. While at Segovia he exchanged it for a regular hair shirt. His hostess found the discarded garment and piously preserved it in a chest. Some time later the house was destroyed by fire, but the chest alone was preserved from the flames. She ascribed this to the merits of Dominic.

Two other happenings connected with Dominic's preaching activity in Segovia are reported by Gerard de Frachet. One day in December, 1218, Dominic preached to a large crowd. Spain was suffering from a severe drought at this time, so that the farmers had not been able to prepare the fields for the winter grain, although it was nearly Christmas. Dominic remembered from his own boyhood what a drought meant to the country, so he prayed to God for relief. At the close of the sermon he encouraged his listeners by telling them that it would soon rain. Very probably some in the audience doubted the fulfillment of the prophecy because the sky was as cloudless as on the preceding days. But Dominic had not been talking nonsense; he cautioned the loiterers to hurry home because the rain would not wait for them. Immediately such a heavy downpour began that the slow-footed were drenched to the skin.

Another incident of this time concerns a meeting attended by Dominic at which a letter from the King was published. After much time had been spent in explanations, Dominic arose and said: "Until now you have listened to the commands of an earthly, mortal king; give a hearing now to the exhortations of the heavenly, immortal King." Thereupon a knight complained angrily "that this pious babbler [Dominic] should prate at us and keep us from our dinner!" As he mounted his horse and rode away, Dominic called after him: "Ride away now, but before a year passes your horse will no longer carry its present master. In vain will you try to escape from your pursuers." Before a year was up the knight was murdered at the selfsame spot where he had belittled Dominic.

Tradition also relates astonishing facts concerning Dominic's devotions and austerities at Segovia. There was a grotto outside the city to which he retired for his prayers and mortifications. It seems that he preferred this grotto to the church in order to conceal the raptures he often experienced in his prayers. For the same reason he scourged himself in the cavern, where the walls didn't have ears. The inhabitants of Segovia did not know that the Saint's life of prayer and mortification was the source of his sermons' efficacy. At the close of 1218, or at the latest by the beginning of 1219, the foundation was far enough advanced to allow the Founder to entrust its completion to other hands. It is usually the financial side of a project that causes the manager's severest headaches. Since the brethren were to live on alms, there was no further need of Dominic's presence.

The case was different in Madrid, where the monastery received both sisters and brothers. There donations in the form of lands and revenues were necessary. The Primate of Spain, Archbishop Rodrigo of Toledo, showed his interest by giving a house to the community, and in the following May a private family gave them an estate. Of course, there were also days when dark clouds gathered. In Guadalajara, north of Madrid, a number of disciples turned their backs on Dominic; only Brother Adam and two lay brothers remained. In words which remind us of Christ's question when at the promise of the Holy Eucharist many incredulous disciples abandoned Him, Dominic asked the three stouthearted, "Will you also go away?" Brother Adam answered in Peter's fashion, "Be it far from me that I should desert the head in order to follow the feet!"

How dearly Dominic cherished the foundation in Madrid is seen in the fact that the only letter extant written by him is addressed to the Sisters there. It bespeaks a stern, sober spirit, intent on the essentials, and warning against the dangers liable to cause disturbances in a community of nuns. The letter reads:

"Brother Dominic, Master of the Preaching Brethren, to the Mother Prioress and the entire community of Sisters in Madrid, greetings and progress in virtue through the grace of God. I praise and thank God for your fervor in the religious life, and that he has called you from the quicksands of the world. My daughters, combat the old enemy by prayer and fasting because only they shall be crowned who have fought lawfully. Hitherto you were deprived of a house adapted for the execution of all our Order's prescriptions, but now that excuse no longer holds good because by the grace of God you have come into possession of a house in which every syllable of the Rule can be carried out. Therefore it is my desire that in the future, silence be observed in all places enjoined by the Constitutions, in the choir, refectory, corridors, and dormitory, and that community life be carried on according to the Constitutions. No one of you shall step beyond the cloister door; no extern shall be admitted, except the Bishop and the Order's Superiors to preach or make a canonical visitation. Do not turn your back on penitential practices and night vigils. Obey your Prioress. Do not waste time in idle gossip. Because I am unable to give you a helping hand in your financial difficulties

I forbid, in order to prevent further distress, that any Brother receive novices without the consent of the Prioress and Sisters. I commission Brother Mannes, who has already done so much for your Monastery and has gathered you into this holy community, to take whatever steps he judges necessary to secure the continuance of your devout life. He has authority to make a visitation of the Convent, to settle what he finds amiss, and, if necessary, to change the Prioress with the consent of the majority of Sisters. According to his discretion he can also dispense from the various austerities. Live holily in Christ."

At Palencia, where Dominic had made his philosophical and theological studies, he now began negotiations for a foundation, convinced that many vocations would develop among the university students. In order to promote this and other plans for propagating the Order in his homeland, he procured a letter of recommendation from the Pope to the Spanish bishops under date of November 15, 1219. Spain was destined to become a flourishing province, but other hands would reap the fruit of Dominic's labors.

PARIS

Paris, with its large and influential University, was an intellectual attraction Dominic could not resist. The seven brethren appointed to Paris were not to travel there in one group, but in two divisions, journeying by different routes. In the first group we find Mannes, the brother germane of Dominic, Brother Michael of Tobra and the lay brother Oderic of Normandy. Traveling ahead by the shortest route they reached Paris on September 12, 1217, and found shelter in the Hospice of the Holy Virgin, a rooming house for travelers. Mannes, the leader of the group, immediately began hunting for a permanent residence, but all his efforts come to nothing. Three weeks later the second group arrived, composed of Matthew of France, Bertrand of Garrigua, John of Navarre, and Lawrence of England. Dominic had arranged for the two latter to continue their studies at the University and John had also to deepen his confidence in God's providence, because in spite of Dominic's pleading, he had refused to set out on the journey without a few coins in his pocket. He seemed to be one of those people who know the world too well to trust it, and God not well enough to rely on Him for their daily bread.

Before dispersing the brethren, Dominic had asked them to elect one of their number who would become Superior in case of his own death. They chose Matthew of France, who had formerly held the office of Prior of the Augustinian Canons at Castres. He took the title of Abbot and remains the only member of the Order to have borne it. In Paris he took over Mannes' work of acquiring a house, but without results. By a strange paradox, a large number of University students and professors were begging admission to the Order, so Abbot Matthew really found himself on the horns of a dilemma; vocations were plentiful, but where house them? After having checked all prospective benefactors from his list, beginning with the Archbishop and continuing on down to the last prosperous businessman, he decided in April, 1218, to send Brothers Bertrand and John of Navarre to Dominic and tell him of the deadlock. Dominic turned for help to the Pope. Honorius ordered the University to procure a home for the brethren. Thereupon Professor John de Barrastre gave them a house and chapel dedicated to St. James near the gate of Orleans. On August 6, 1218, Matthew and his companions took up residence and began community life according to the Rule of St. Augustine and the Constitutions of the Order of Preachers, but the Archbishop would not permit them to conduct public services in their church. The priests of St. Benedict's parish seem to have put the Archbishop up to this because they feared a diminution of their own church attendance. The brethren had lived eleven months in rented quarters, waiting for a house of their own. Now they had to wait eight more months before the privilege of public worship in their own church was granted.

In the meantime, Dominic was in Spain. On the journey to Paris, which he made on foot, he had visited Prouille and Toulouse and found the Crusaders' fortunes in rather bad shape. The

French Crown Prince was besieging Toulouse in a hopeless effort to expel Raymond. Dominic's confidence in God strengthened the brothers and sisters to hold on no matter how hard pressed.

In July Dominic came to Paris. The increase in numbers from seven brethren to thirty must have been gratifying to him. Most of the new recruits were from the University's intellectual circle. Probably some of the earlier members felt a little out of place among these giants of learning, like Peter Seila, the former merchant, who had given the Order its first house at Toulouse and whose only book was a solitary copy of St. Gregory's Homilies. The fact that the community lived in perfect harmony in spite of the differences between the pioneer members and the newer set is quite a tribute to Abbot Matthew's ability as a superior. Soon after Dominic's arrival, the house was agog; thirty brethren in one place was too much, so he would scatter the seed to prevent its decay. In two months' time he had dispersed groups of two and three to make foundations at Limoges, Rheims, Metz, Poitiers, and Orleans. The only complaint at Paris was that they could not conduct public services in their church. In this unpleasant situation help must again be sought from the Pope. Dominic felt certain of winning his point; the Pope had approved them as Canons according to the Rule of St. Augustine, and a Church with public worship is a priority of every Augustinian Monastery. On December 1, 1219, the Pope decided the question in favor of the brethren.

The University Chancellor and the priors of St. Dionysius and St. Germanus were charged to see that the privilege was respected. Many discussions followed about the indemnification due to the parish of St. Benedict, but the doors of St. James were open to numerous worshipers. It seems that the pastor of St. Benedict's never got over his disgruntled feelings, because he snarled at the Preaching Brethren on every occasion and in every sermon.

Dominic obtained another important document from the Pope on December 12 in behalf of the sorely tried community in Paris. Therein we read: "Because in the strength of the Holy Spirit you have cast off all temporal possessions in order to dedicate yourselves to the task of announcing the Gospel in perfect poverty, and have already endured many hardships and dangers for this purpose, we confidently trust that your labors will produce much fruit. In our desire of encouraging you in this salutary undertaking, we grant you our apostolic benediction."

During his stay in Paris Dominic received into the Order William of Montferrat, whom he had met two years previously at the home of Cardinal Ugolino in Rome. William was so enraptured by Dominic's zeal for the conversion of the Cuman Tartars that he wanted to join the Order immediately, but Dominic had advised him to continue his theological studies for two years at the University of Paris, thinking this would give him time to regulate the affairs of the Order and permit him to set out with his young disciple for the foreign missions. Even though after two years the Order was not sufficiently stabilized to permit the Founder's prolonged absence, William nevertheless joined the Preaching Brethren and became a faithful companion of his spiritual father on many treks across Europe.

On one occasion when Dominic preached a sermon to the students of the University of Paris, there was in the audience a young man by the name of Jordan, from Saxony, who later made his confession to the preacher and asked his spiritual guidance. Dominic counseled him to receive diaconate orders, but Jordan held back because he was plagued by the fear that perfect chastity was beyond his strength. While visiting Bologna several months later, Dominic sent from there to Paris Brother Reginald, one of those vibrant personalities who magnetize whatever profession they embrace. Bologna was loathe to lose this forcible preacher, whose sermons had accomplished much good in souls. In Paris, his sphere of influence was widened; he won many vocations to the Order, among them Jordan and his friend, Henry of Marsberg, whose eloquence held Paris spellbound. Unfortunately, Reginald died on February 1, 1220, before his talents were fully unfolded.

BOLOGNA

The world-renowned School of Canon Law attached to the University of Bologna was another silver hook attracting the Founder of an ecumenical Preaching Order, because as student and teacher the Friar Preacher must choose those cities which afford the best opportunity for learning and lecturing. On his journeys from France to Rome, Dominic had passed through Bologna and received hospitality in an Augustinian Canonry at Mascarella, a suburb of the city. There had not been enough brethren to send a detachment to Bologna at the dispersal of August 15, 1217; but the foundation became a reality in spite of this handicap since, during an earlier journey, Dominic had interested several Bolognese in the projected Order. With these he made a beginning in 1218. An elderly priest, Richard the Senior, was appointed superior, and the Canons of Mascarella offered a section of their monastery to accommodate these pioneer Dominicans, Dominic himself did not remain long with them; the Order's concerns were calling him to Rome. But he kept in close contact with the newly formed community and sent them fresh recruits. Although the community at Mascarella increased in numbers, an important factor was lacking, a master spirit to give it prestige. But Divine Providence would provide; as a matter of fact, the seed had already been planted and was now flowering in the person of Reginald of Orleans.

Reginald had taught Canon Law at the University of Paris from 1206 to 1212, when he was elected dean of the Augustinian Canons at Orleans, an office which carried with it a generous share of feudal wealth and privileges. But instead of experiencing peace and satisfaction, Reginald now endured that consistent inconsistency which worldly success so often stirs up in the souls of those called to higher achievements. A taste of temporal wealth and knowledge made him realize that he had been created for better things.

In 1218 Bishop Manasses, noticing the strange depression which had come over the learned Dean, chose him as companion on a pilgrimage to Rome and the Holy Land, thinking that a diversion would cheer up his spirits. Through Cardinal Ugolino's introduction at Rome, Reginald met Dominic and was so captivated by his plans that he decided to join the Order. Dominic saw in him the very man necessary for the Bologna community. Just at this crucial time Reginald became deathly sick, his illness caused perhaps by the violent struggle between nature and grace going on in his soul. Dominic stormed heaven, asking God to spare him, at least for a time, this son so indispensable for his work. Heaven answered. While Dominic was in church praying, Reginald had a vision in which the Mother of God came to his sickbed and anointed him. He was cured. Mary then showed him the habit of the Order, not to induce him to enter, because he was already determined to do so, but to tell him she wanted a slight change made in the habit worn by the brethren at that time. Instead of the Canon's rochet, they should adopt a white woolen scapular. Reginald was received into the Order by Dominic, accompanied his Bishop to Palestine, and returned toward the close of 1218 to begin his activities at Bologna. Jordan thus describes his fervor: "His eloquence was like a glowing torch, setting on fire the hearts of his hearers. All Bologna was in flames. It seemed as if a new Elias were traversing the city." His appeal was not merely to the rank and file who always hang on a new preacher's words, but it was especially to the University faculty and students, who were ignited by this spiritual firebrand. Three of the most influential professors joined the Order: Clarus Sesto, Paul of Venice, and Guala of Bergamo.

All this time at Mascarella the brethren were living in rented quarters. Richard's efforts to acquire a suitable dwelling had been fruitless. Reginald considered the suburban location of Mascarella a hindrance to his preaching activity, so he began to look around for a monastery within the city. With the Archbishop's consent the Church of St. Nicholas was given to the Brethren by its rector Rudolph, who also entered the Order. Soon afterward Lovellos d'Andallo gave to the community the land and houses near the Church. This gift was inspired by Lovellos' daughter, Dianna, a high-born and high-spirited young lady, whom grace had touched and transformed by means of Reginald's discourses on sacred doctrine.

Gerard de Frachet gives a striking example of Reginald's recruiting ability. His preaching had won so many students to the Order that the Professor of Philosophy, Moneta of Cremona, began to fear that he would himself succumb to the preacher's persuasion. Not only did he avoid meeting Reginald, but he also tried to alienate the students from him. On St. Stephen's Feast some of them invited Moneta to go with them to St. Nicholas in order to hear Reginald. Not wanting to decline the invitation outright, he coaxed them first to attend Mass with him at St. Proclus, and then cleverly remained there long enough to feel certain that Reginald's sermon was over. We are not told whether Reginald was habitually long-winded, but at least that day he spoke longer than Moneta had anticipated. When they reached St. Nicholas, the densely packed church allowed them just to squeeze inside the doorway. Moneta heard Reginald's full-toned voice calling out: "I see the heavens open! Yes, open for those who want to enter. Lukewarm and sluggish souls, do not shut your heart, your mouth, your hands, lest heaven close on you. My friends, what are you waiting for?" These few words gripped and transformed Moneta's soul. Immediately after the sermon he pushed his way through the crowd to Reginald and promised to enter the Order. Because his duties as professor could not immediately be resigned, he continued another year at his post; but, just as he had previously cautioned others not to attend Reginald's sermons, now he encouraged everybody to listen to him. After a year's interval he entered the Order.

It was customary at that period for aspirants to enter religious life on the spur of the moment;

consequently there were also many desertions and even days of melancholy and uncertainty about the very existence of the Community. Gerard relates such an incident. Brothers Theobald of Siena and Nicholas of Campania had become disgruntled and obtained from Cardinal Ugolino permission to transfer to the Cistercian Order. Reginald informed the assembled community of their decision. If he expected that the majority would disapprove of the decision and thereby the two malcontents would be moved to repentance, he was mistaken. Master Clarus arose and tried to calm the storm of discouragement, but it was like preaching to the wind. Then the door of the chapter room opened and the University's most renowned professor, Roland of Cremona, entered and earnestly begged to be clothed in the habit of the Order. Reginald was so overjoyed that without waiting for a new habit to be brought, he cast his own capuche on the petitioner's head. All despondency melted away, and the two would-be Cistercians tore up their transfer letter and vowed anew to persevere in the Order until death.

Dominic frequently visited Bologna for the purpose of keeping tab on the community's progress. All his hopes were realized in Reginald, who rounded out the community's external development and interior spirit in a very short time. It is not stretching the truth to say that Reginald was necessary for the Order because his firmness counterbalanced Dominic's mildness.

Another motive often calling Dominic to

Bologna was his concern for Dianna, the daughter of Lovellos d'Andallo. Dianna, highly intellectual and well aware of her physical and mental attractiveness, had been captivated by Reginald's lectures. She was introduced to Dominic and revealed to him her desire to serve God in the Order of Preachers. Dominic saw in her the person who would be able to establish in Bologna a citadel of contemplation and regular observance such as had already been formed in Prouille, so he allowed her to make in his presence a twofold vow of virginity and to enter the Order as soon as a Convent would be established in Bologna. But her family had other plans and tried to change her mind by fair means and foul. In an effort to keep her vow as far as possible, Dianna secretly entered a Benedictine Abbey from which her brothers removed her so forcibly that several of her ribs were broken. She was then imprisoned in her home and forbidden any communication with the Dominicans, but by a holy stealth Dominic sent her letters of counsel and encouragement. It was only after Dominic's death that Dianna escaped from her domestic confinement and again expressed her determination of becoming a Dominican. This time her parents softened and Dominic's successor as Master General, Jordan of Saxony, helped her found the Convent of St. Agnes in Bologna.

ROME

When dispersing the brethren on the feast of Mary's Assumption, 1217, Dominic chose Rome as focus of his own travels for two reasons: in order to renew the Pope's protection for the harrowed foundations at Prouille and Toulouse, and to establish a fortress of truth at the center of Christianity. His former association with Bishops Diego and Faulke had put him on friendly terms with several influential cardinals, and a number of young men had expressed their desire of joining the Order. Very probably Pope Honorius himself encouraged Dominic to open in the Eternal City a house of the Order whose particular mission is the preaching of God's Word to all nations. Honorius also had in mind a commission which he would later expressly entrust to Dominic.

Pope Innocent III had adopted a practical plan of church reform. In the Trastevere there was an Abbey of Benedictine nuns whose religious life left much to be desired. The cloister was not observed; the community held lavish open house for its wealthy friends and benefactors, and the nuns went on frequent vacations to their families and relatives. The vow of poverty was just a polite phrase to these highborn ladies. In order to improve matters effectively, Innocent planned to move the community to a different locality and give the nuns a new Rule. He had a monastery built near the Church of San Sisto where they were to live a life worthy of their high calling under the direction of the Gilbertine Fathers. At the time of Innocent's death the building was not complete and the Gilbertines had not taken up their charge, nor did they ever do so. In the finished section, with the help of disciples enlisted in Rome, Dominic laid the foundations of his first Roman Monastery.

When Dominic visited the Papal Curia at Viterbo in 1219, Honorius commissioned him with the reform of the Sisters and their transfer from Trastevere to San Sisto. To compensate the brethren for the loss of their Convent, Honorius gave them one of the Savelli palaces on the Aventine, the same one, by a twist of Providence, where he had signed the Bull of Approval several years before. This monastery of the Preaching Brethren came to be known as Santa Sabina. Dominic did not pigeonhole this assignment, which was the answer to his prayers for a monastery of Brothers, and one of Sisters, in the Eternal City. As representative of the Pope he informed the nuns of the transfer and reform of their community. At first he received nothing but rebuffs, for these ladies of leisure had no intention of exchanging their enjoyable life for the cold asceticism Dominic set before them. Eventually some of the nuns, touched by grace, agreed to go to San Sisto and they renewed their religious vows; but when news of the forthcoming departure was noised abroad in the city, their relatives blew up a cyclone against the Spanish monk and induced those who had agreed to go to recall their promise of leaving the Trastevere. But Dominic was not discouraged. He addressed a spiritual conference to the nuns and at its close asked those who wanted to go to San Sisto to renew their vows. All did so on one condition, that they be permitted to take with them the miraculous picture of the Mother of God. If this picture would return to the Trastevere (as had happened once before), they would also return. Dominic agreed to the proposal, but fearing the undesirable influx of relatives, he stationed lay brothers on guard at the monastery gate and along the way.

The transfer took place on Ash Wednesday, 1220. In order to add solemnity to the event, Cardinals Ugolino from Ostia, Stephen from Fossanova, and Nicholas from Tuscany awaited the community at San Sisto. While the nuns, directed by Dominic and guarded by the lay brothers, approached the new monastery and were greeted by the cardinals, the horse of Cardinal Stephen's nephew became frightened and threw its rider. The man's body was carried to the monastery and with characteristic feminine repercussion the terrified Sisters immediately cried out: "Is this a sign God doesn't approve of our decision?" Brother Tankret, the prior of the brethren, chided Dominic: "What are you waiting for? Why don't you call on God? Where is now your compassion for your neighbor and your confidence in God?" Stirred by this admonition, Dominic had the body brought into a room, which he then locked. After celebrating Mass he restored the young man to life and led him out, sound of mind and limb. As a result of this miracle the nuns willingly adjusted themselves to their new environment. Dominic had summoned four nuns from Prouille to initiate the Benedictines in the spirit of the new Order. The former Abbess resigned her office and Sister Blanche from Prouille was elected Prioress. Before long nuns from other relaxed Convents who desired to live a life of contemplation joined the community so that the number increased to forty-five. All made profession in the hands of their new spiritual Father and promised to strive after intense holiness. Cecilia Cesarini, the youngest of the sisters from Trastevere, testified to these facts in her old age and avowed that she made profession to Dominic on three different occasions.

The community's material needs were well provided for because Pope Honorius had given to the Sisters all the revenues of the monastery in Trastevere. This lightened the responsibility of the brethren charged with the temporalities of the monastery; only as many as were needed to look after the spiritual and material needs of the Sisters remained at San Sisto. Even though the buildings on the Aventine were not legally transferred to the brethren until 1222, it is certain that they resided at Santa Sabina before that date because a small room, now transformed into a chapel, served as a cell for Dominic, who died in 1221.

The political situation in Rome at this time was not fertile soil for the growth of the Preaching Brethren. The disturbances instigated by Senator Terentius kept the city in such turmoil that Pope Honorius had gone to Viterbo with the Papal Curia. Dominic and his brethren preached to the people but with very little success in the way of moral transformation; and almsgiving was equally meager. Nevertheless, the Founder held fast to his ideal of perfect poverty and God assisted him miraculously. Blessed Cecilia states that at the time when the brethren still lived at San Sisto and the Sisters at Trastevere, the brethren one day returned empty-handed from their begging expedition. When mealtime came Dominic ordered that the bell be rung summoning the brethren to the refectory. This was done, although perhaps with some misgivings. As they were seated at table, feasting their eyes on the floor boards, the door suddenly swung open and two young men entered carrying bread in snowy white cloths. Beginning with the youngest brother and proceeding to Dominic, they laid a loaf at each one's place and then disappeared as mysteriously as they had come. Dominic said to the brethren: "Eat the bread which the Lord has provided!" Then he sent the procurator to get wine from the cellar. To their great astonishment the previously empty keg was now filled with good wine. Cecilia herself ate some of the miraculous bread because the brethren shared their good fortune with the Sisters. This miracle, which strengthened the brethren's confidence in Divine Providence, is not the only incident of supernatural assistance recorded of Dominic's lifetime.

Dominic loved to visit the Sisters at San Sisto during intervals between his apostolic journeys. Sister Cecilia relates that one time he arrived at the monastery after the Sisters had retired for the night. Nevertheless, he had the bell rung calling them to a conference on the spiritual life. The instruction ended, he told the Sister procuratrix to bring some wine, saying that after the spirit is refreshed, the body should also be provided for. The Prioress explained that they had only a cupful of wine in the house, which they were saving for the sick. But Dominic ordered the cup to be passed around and when the brethren and Sisters had all taken as much as they pleased, the supply remained undiminished. Since it was already late in the evening they begged their spiritual Father to spend the night at San Sisto, but he said he must return to Santa Sabina. The two Brothers stationed at the Convent determined to accompany him, so that no harm would befall him in the unquiet city. What was their astonishment when they saw a young man standing at the gate, apparently waiting for them, who preceded them to Santa Sabina, unlocked the door without a key, and then vanished into the night air!

If Dominic had wanted to rest on his oars, the two Roman monasteries would have served as excellent props for human satisfaction. At San Sisto Pope Innocent's reform of relaxed sisterhoods had been accomplished, while at Santa Sabina the Lateran Council's decrees concerning the preaching of divine truth were being fulfilled. Chances are, however, that the man whom God had used as instrument in these projects was too busy making plans for the Order's development to waste his time in self-applause.

VI

THE EXPANSION OF THE ORDER

THE INNER DEVELOPMENT

DURING the four years which had elapsed since the Order's approval it had been conducted on the trial and error basis. An attempt had been made to realize the ideal set forth in the Rule and Constitutions, but serious differences of opinion had arisen, so Dominic decided to confer with the brethren whether certain changes and modifications should be made in the Constitutions. Representatives from the individual houses convened at Bologna on Pentecost Sunday, 1220, in response to the Founder's rallying cry. From Paris came four delegates, among them Jordan of Saxony who had just recently received the habit. We are indebted to him for en famille points concerning this first General Chapter of the Order of Preachers. At the opening session Dominic begged the brethren to relieve him of the government of the Order because he considered himself unfitted for that post and wanted to preach the faith to the Cuman Tartars; but they turned a deaf ear to this petition. Thereupon Dominic appealed to the Board of Definitions that he be divested, at least for the duration of the Chapter, of the highest authority, which depended during those days on this Board.

They agreed to this proposal and then appointed Dominic himself as chairman of the five members composing the Board.

No change being necessary in the Order's purpose — the salvation of mankind by preaching the gospel truths — the consultation began with a sifting of the type of poverty to be practiced. Until then the Order had owned property, had accepted revenues, and had permitted the brethren to take money on their journeys, even though Dominic himself never did so and permitted it only very unwillingly — as with John of Navarre. Dominic still looked at poverty from the same angle as he had in the days of Diego. He repeated at the conference his principle that perfect poverty in the preacher is a continuous, wordless sermon, and that without this powerful example preaching is liable to be nothing but din in the ears. He considered poverty as an essential means to study and preaching, and suggested that the Order, as well as the individual members, should observe absolute poverty. On this point he met with thorny opposition, especially from the procurators, who said that they often did not know where to turn for the community's next meal. After much interchange of views and a little word fencing, an agreement was reached; the Order could possess property such as churches, monasteries, and grounds, but ownership of extensive estates and buildings was to be renounced. Concerning revenues it was decided that no more were to be accepted in the future; the brethren should exist on the alms offered them on the occasion of their preaching or by outright begging. Traveling money was denied them; being permitted to preach everywhere, they should also everywhere live on alms. In the execution of these prescriptions the property in southern France was transferred to the Nuns at Prouille and Toulouse, in Spain to the Nuns at Madrid, in Italy to San Sisto, and in northern France to religious women of other orders. Dominic also renounced the revenues previously deeded to the Order; even the tithes granted by Bishop Faulke he would no longer accept. In presence of the assembled brethren the Founder tore up a contract very favorable to the Order because it was at variance with this viewpoint.

New strength was given the vow of obedience by the resolution that profession was not to be made to the local superior, as was customary among the Augustinian Canons, but to the highest superior of the Order. This master stroke cut off the members from attachment to a particular house and made them subject to the highest superior, bound by vow to go wherever he commanded. Dominic had already acted in this way when dispersing the first brethren, but now it was established as the lawful procedure for future generations of Preaching Brethren. This centralization would prove beneficial to the Order because it placed the talents of all members at the disposal of the Master General, as the highest superior was hereafter called, to be employed by him wherever necessary. The *stabilitas loci* — "stability of place" — of the older monks, herein contrasted by the *mobilitas fratrum* — "movable brethren" — was a source of astonishment to many. But it was necessary for the Order's world-wide mission, and was also spiritually helpful to the individual because it released him from the inordinate or merely natural attachments, and made the soul ready to go to the end of the world if God so willed.

In regard to the Divine Office it was decided that the chant should be brisk. This resolution also caused more than one monk and canon to raise their eyebrows; however, the decision was not motivated by depreciation of the Church's official prayer, but by interest in the Order's purpose. It was intended to give the brethren more time for study and preaching. Even the monastic Orders shortened choral prayer during the harvest season.

Then Dominic called the attention of the assembled brethren to the white woolen scapular which the Mother of God had given to Reginald in Rome with the words, "Behold the habit of thine Order." He noticed that some of those present were not wearing it, although in his visitations of the various houses he had repeatedly expressed the wish that they adopt it in place of the canons' rochet. So he then and there ordained unconditionally that the white scapular was to be thereafter the sign by which Dominicans would be known by the whole world as the devoted children of Mary. This smothered the criticisms of certain skeptical brethren about the "visions of a delirious man."

The subject of education was also opened for an interchange of views. The arrangement at St. James in Paris, where Professor John of Barrastre, who had joined the Brethren after giving them a suitable monastery, now conducted courses in theology and holy scripture which the priests as well as the students were obliged to attend, was held up to the assembly as a model by Dominic. It was decided that in future no monastery should be founded without a prior and lector. The very title of the Order's highest superior, "Master General," shows how impregnated the brethren were with study as their first principle, which, although not the Order's immediate purpose, is absolutely necessary for the attainment of that purpose - preaching and saving of souls — which cannot be achieved without study.

It was also decided to hold a Chapter every year, alternating between Bologna and Paris, the next one to be held again at Bologna because the monastery in Paris was not yet large enough to accommodate such a numerous assembly.

The year 1220-1221 was of great consequence to the Order, both in regard to the reception of new members and the establishment of many monasteries. The centralization which had been decreed the previous year, whereby each member engaged himself directly to the Master General to be disposed of as he deemed best for the Order, would have proved satisfactory in a small organization spread over a limited territory. But when foundations were made in distant countries, the centralization had to be modified and supplemented because it was impossible for one man to know personally all these subjects, or to be fully acquainted with the needs of various countries.

The General Chapter which convened at St. Nicholas in Bologna at Pentecost, 1221, was faced with the problem of dividing the Order into provinces. It was decided to group the monasteries of one country into an administrative district to be governed by a provincial superior who had to render an account of his steerage to the Master General; thus the central authority remained intact. Every individual brother, no matter where he was stationed, had the privilege of addressing himself directly to the Master General. The purpose of thus dividing the Order into provinces was to unburden the Master General of minor details, to make sure that every member's talents were given the opportunity for development, and to promote the Order's expansion.

The monasteries in Spain were formed into the Spanish Province, those of southern France into the Provencal province, those of northern France into the French province, those of central Italy into the Roman province, and those of upper Italy into the Lombard province. Because houses had already been established in Germany and Hungary, the formation of these into provinces was planned; even England was considered, although the first

English monastery of the Order had yet to be opened. This General Chapter of 1221 also appointed the superiors for these eight provinces. As provincial for Spain it named Suero of Gomez, the companion of Peter of Madrid who had previously returned despondent to Dominic. For Provence it designated Bertrand of Garrigua, whom we are told Dominic advised not to weep so much for his own sins, but for the iniquity of mankind.

Bertrand had been present when, at a Sign of the Cross made by Dominic, they passed through a rainstorm without becoming wet; and he also shared in the gift of tongues, when he, with Dominic, was able miraculously to preach to some German pilgrims, who had given the friars material provisions. Peter of Rheims was appointed to the French province and Master Clarus to the Roman province. The provinces of Germany, Hungary, and England each received a native son as provincial: Conrad the German, Paul of Hungary, and Gilbert of England. Jordan of Saxony, who was not present at this Second Chapter, was named provincial of upper Italy. The appointment took away his breath because, being so young in religion, he considered it more necessary for him to give ear than give orders. Nevertheless, he immediately left Paris, where he received the assignment, in company with an older brother Everard, who had won quite a few temporal laurels before joining the Order and had even been offered a bishopric. Everard's greatest desire in the Order was to know the Founder personally. In order to satisfy Everard's wish, Jordan chose him as traveling companion. They crossed the Alps to Lausanne, where Everard became sick and died. Although his longing to see Dominic was not fulfilled on earth, his desire indicates the importance of the Founder in relation to his work. Although the Rule and Constitutions bound the members into a unit and they strove for a common ideal, it was love for the Founder which formed the tenderest and strongest bond between them. Everard died peacefully. He scolded his attendants for trying to hide the fact that death was at his heels: "Why try to keep secret what I so earnestly long for!"

Jordan continued his journey to the Lombard plain. There lay waiting for him the field of labor in which he was to represent the Founder whom he venerated so highly. Jordan proved his mettle. Within a year's time he was destined to replace Dominic as Master General. It is difficult to understand what made the brethren choose this rather shy young priest, except that his character resembled Dominic's most closely, especially in those gifts by which, as Master General, he would have to hold the Order together. He had the same energetic physical make-up and the ability to influence those under him to put forth their best efforts. His personal charm and tact, united to his eloquence as a preacher, drew his hearers to him, especially the students of whatever congregation he addressed.

At the second General Chapter Dominic did not renew his petition to be relieved from office in order to go on the foreign missions. He knew that his candle was burning low and he foretold his early death to a group of students whom he was addressing in Bologna. This presentiment did not harrow his soul; the Order of Preachers, his brain child, was established on the unchangeable rock of truth.

EXTERIOR PROPAGATION

Basing our statement on the early chronicles of the Order, we may say that Dominic was generously blessed with that mixture of charm and reserve which attracts and holds men's hearts. Stephen the Spaniard deposed at the canonization process that he was among the students who listened to Dominic at Bologna in 1220 and felt attracted by his gentleness. One evening shortly after he had heard Dominic preach and as Stephen was about to eat supper with his companions, Dominic sent two brethren with the message, "Brother Dominic bids Stephen come to him immediately." Stephen played for a little time. "I will come as soon as I have finished my meal," he told the messengers. But they insisted that Dominic had emphasized the word, immediately. So Stephen arose and went to St. Nicholas Church, where Dominic and the community met him, Dominic told one of the brethren to show him how to make the *venia*—the act of prostrating oneself on the floor, as a sign of humility and penance. As Stephen arose from the venia, Dominic extended his hands to him. Before he could step back, Dominic had placed on his shoulders the habit of the Preaching Brethren, saying, "I present you with the weapons wherewith you must combat the devil throughout your lifetime." Stephen did not know what to make of this unheard-of procedure, since he had not mentioned his vocation to Dominic; but he supposed that the Founder had acted thus by divine inspiration.

Constantine of Orvieto tells us that the brethren in Bologna were bent upon gaining Conrad the German, a professor at the University, for the Order. On Assumption Eve, 1220, Dominic was talking at St. Nicholas with a visiting Cistercian monk, prior of the monastery in Casamare, and he said to him: "Prior, I hereby tell you what I have never told anyone else, and I beg you to keep it in strict confidence until my death. God has never refused me anything I asked of Him in prayer." Knowing of the brethren's desire concerning Master Conrad, the prior replied: "If that is so, Father, why do you not ask God to give Master Conrad to the Order?" Dominic answered: "My dear Brother, you now mention something that is difficult of attainment. But if you will join me in prayer during this night, I feel certain that God will grant our petition." After Compline, Dominic and the Prior remained in choir, prayed until Matins, and afterward continued their private devotions till Prime. As the cantor intoned the hymn of the Church's morning prayer, Master Conrad walked into the choir, knelt before

Dominic, and begged to be clothed in the habit of the Order. This convinced the Prior of the power of Dominic's prayers. He guarded the secret until after the death of Dominic, whom he outlived twenty years.

Stephen the Spaniard tells us that Dominic was a pillar of strength to the brethren undergoing temptations against their vocation. Stephen was talking from experience because his early days in the Order had not been without thorns; but the Founder's encouragement had helped him to surmount all obstacles and keep to his course. In reading the early chronicles we get the impression that Dominic suffered personally at every defection from the Order. His prayers followed the deserters and not infrequently brought them back, ready to turn over a new leaf. John of Salerno is an example. Dominic had gained this promising student for the Order in Bologna and set high hopes on the intelligent, warmhearted brother. However, coming from an aristocratic family, John found religious life too much of a grind after his first enthusiasm had taken wings. Besides this, his relatives kept urging him to return to the world, until he finally gave way. Dominic was deeply distressed and prayed for him. Like many before and after him, John found that the pleasures which had allured him now filled him with loathing, so he returned to Dominic and begged to be again clothed in the habit of the Order. His petition was immediately granted. After this experience John remained true to his vocation and justified the confidence placed in him by Dominic, who sometime later appointed him superior of the brethren sent to found a monastery in Florence, even though he was the youngest of the group. John is numbered among the Blessed of the Order.

Dominic daily addressed a conference to the brethren in order to strengthen them in their vocation and to stir up their zeal for the Order's ideals. The fiery fervor which gripped him during these straight-from-the-shoulder talks sent off sparks which set his hearers ablaze for their own sanctification and the salvation of their fellow men.

Dominic had only five short years in which to spread out his Order. Many monasteries claim the honor of having been established by the Founder himself. This assertion has been challenged by historians, but in the majority of cases the fact is beyond dispute. Blessed Jordan's account of Dominic's establishment of the Madrid and Segovia foundations is uncontested. The establishment in Palencia can trace its origin to him because he made the preliminary preparations and gave a helping hand across the miles. Barcelona, Santarem, and Zamora had similar beginnings. In southern France, Prouille and Toulouse enjoy the honor of having been founded directly by him. Lyons dates back to him; the choice of this city, the headquarters of the Waldensians, and of Montpellier, the stronghold of the Albigensians, is entirely in accord with Dominic's purpose of setting his spiritual family to fight the heretics. According to Dr. Scheeben's researches, Bayonne,

Le Puy, and Narbonne were founded by Dominic. Among the monasteries of northern France, the first place belongs to St. James in Paris, Dominic's trump card. For several centuries this house was the Order's spiritual hub where lectors were trained and sent out to the various provinces in order to make certain that all members were thoroughly grounded in both sacred and secular sciences. No other monastery exerted such influence upon the entire Order as did St. James in Paris — not even St. Nicholas at Bologna nor Santa Sabina at Rome. The foundation at Limoges was prepared by the Founder and rounded out by Brother Peter Seila. Rheims and Orleans also revert to Dominic; in the choice of the latter city the memory of the unforgettable Reginald played an important part. Although the city of Metz is located in Germany, its monastery, which dates back to Dominic, has always been grouped in the French province. In his address of welcome, Bishop Conrad expressed the hope that the brethren would not limit themselves to instructing the laity in Christian principles, but would also hoist the clergy to a higher spiritual level.

In central Italy Dominic made a beginning with San Sisto at Rome. When the brethren vacated San Sisto in favor of the nuns, the second foundation in the Eternal City Santa Sabina — came into existence. In no other place has the memory of the holy Founder remained so alive as in these two monasteries. In northern Italy the first monastery of the Order was erected in Bologna; it was in this city, at St. Nicholas, that Dominic wound up the Order's development in the first two General Chapters, and there also he completed his earthly course. Other Italian monasteries claiming Dominic as their founder are located in Milan, Bergamo, Venice, Pisa, Brescia, Siena, and Florence. Hungary and Germany each have two monasteries dating to the Founder's lifetime: Vesprim and Stuhlweisenberg, Freiberg and Cologne.

To appreciate fully the difficulties involved in the task of founding thirty monasteries within five years, we must remember that the novel aims and methods of the Preaching Brethren were a bugbear to many of Dominic's contemporaries. In the thirteenth century as well as in the twentieth, there were people to whom every new idea gave a headache, and who wouldn't consent to swallow an aspirin of optimism for fear of losing the pleasure of having an ache to complain about.

VII
LIFE'S CLOSE

ILLNESS AND DEATH

DOMINIC GUZMAN is a good proof of the phrase, "Appearances are deceiving." The amount of work he accomplished gives the impression that his physical frame was towering, broad-shouldered, and muscular, but the declarations of his contemporaries plainly contradict such an idea. We have seen how his life of mortification put in the shade all the ostensible penances of the heretical leaders, and that he devoted himself to devotional exercises with an earnestness that could hardly be surpassed. All this was done under the direction of his spiritual faculties at the expense of his physical powers. The question may arise whether Dominic would have accomplished more if he had placed his health under the care of a doctor, eaten suitable nourishment, and taken sufficient rest in a soft bed. Perhaps his lifespan would have been lengthened a few years, but he would have worked less effectually, and the ultimate success of his enterprise would have been jeopardized. The Albigensians would have scornfully said, "He is another one of those slack, neither hot nor cold, canons!" In order to be fair, we must look at the other side of the picture: it is plain fact that thirteenth-century men were not as prone to coddle their bodies and speak of their ailments as we are today. Their supernatural outlook on life buoyed them up in time of illness. If the malady became serious they consulted the doctor and applied his remedies. Dominic was the child of his century. What seems extreme in the way of austerity to twentieth-century eyes was quite the ordinary road seven centuries ago.

After the Second General Chapter in Bologna, Dominic set out for Venice where he made preliminary arrangements for a foundation. Cardinal Ugolino was just then in the same city directing plans for a fresh Crusade, so Dominic sought him out and confided to him the results of the recent Chapter. In mid-July he returned to Bologna, arriving at St. Nicholas after nightfall. He was fagged out from the heat of an Italian summer, but conferred a long time with Prior Ventura and Procurator Rudolph about the affairs of the house. As midnight approached, the two tried to persuade him not to attend Matins but to take what sleep he could. Thinking they had gained the point, they themselves went to bed and learned next day that Dominic, on leaving them, had gone to midnight Matins. Participation in that night's Matins was the last community exercise at which he assisted. A racking headache and violent fever forced him to take some rest until the hour of Prime. In the morning he inquired about different community matters and expressed satisfaction that the cells, which had been built too large, had been made smaller. On a previous visit he had taken the procurator to task: "Will you begin to build palaces already in my lifetime?" When Cardinal Ugolino came to Bologna at the end of July, Dominic gathered his remaining strength and visited his spiritual daughter, Dianna. Since he could not speak with her long, and only in the presence of the Cardinal and her parents, he had to limit himself to a few hurried words of encouragement in her vocation. This was his last activity in the interest of the Sisters' branch of the Order.

The beginning of August brought a severe decline in his condition. The intense heat of the city added to the discomforts of the fever, so the brethren decided to carry him to a rectory adjoining the Church of the Holy Virgin in the city's suburb. He had been there only a day when the rector made a remark to some of the brethren about burying their Founder in his church. They were panic-stricken and, by force of habit, asked their Father what his choice was in the matter. Dominic answered in his usual, unvarnished style: "Under the feet of my brethren!" He instructed them to carry him quickly back to their own monastery so that the rector would have no claim upon his body. As they carried him back to the city, his weakness was so apparent that they were afraid he might die on the way.

Realizing that life was fast failing him, Dominic had asked for the sacrament of Extreme Unction while in the rectory of the Church of the Holy Virgin. Prior Ventura performed this last anointing in the presence of twenty brethren.

Gathering together his rapidly ebbing strength, the Founder mused over the past and gave an inkling of the inner clash of arms none had ever surmised. "God has mercifully kept me to this day in pure and unstained virginity. If you desire this blessed gift from God, keep away from everything that can conjure up evil, for it is by watchful care in this that a man is loved by God and revered by man." But chastity, the lily among virtues, must be hedged in by silence and humility; so his next words were of self-reproach and a plea that they remember him not as an Elysian being beyond imitation, but a fallible mortal like themselves, at sea in a leaky vessel. "Though God's grace has preserved me from stain till this moment, I must admit that I took more pleasure in conversation with young women than with old." Then his voice became almost inaudible and, as if scrupling over such an admission, he whispered to the Prior, "I think I have done wrong in speaking so openly of my chastity. It would have been wiser to keep the King's secrets silent."

It seems almost absurd to speak of the Last Testament of a mendicant friar, dying in another's bed because he had none of his own. But Dominic made such a bequest, leaving to his spiritual family the all of his nothingness. "Beloved sons, this is the patrimony I leave you. Have charity one for another, hold fast to humility, make your treasure out of voluntary poverty." Humbert the Roman, Dominic's fourth successor as Master General, read between the lines of this unique legacy: "Oh

Testament of peace, oh memorable, unchangeable, and priceless Testament! Testament, I say, made effective not through the death of the testator, but by his arrival at eternal life. Blessed is he who does not cast aside the timeless garment of charity, who digs deep in the fertile soil of humility, who rightly appraises the priceless treasure of poverty, this legacy of such an illustrious Father!"

Dominic was still alive when they brought him back to St. Nicholas. After a few hours he said to the Prior and brethren, "Keep yourselves in readiness!" Prior Ventura spoke in the name of all: "Father, you know how sad and lonely your death will leave us. Remember us in prayer before God." Dominic raised his hands and prayed: "Holy Father, thou knowest I have always protected and preserved the souls Thou gavest me. I recommend them to Thee; do Thou guard and guide them!" To the brethren who begged him to keep them in his care, he said, "I will be more useful to you after my death than during life." Shortly after this he addressed the Prior, "Begin the prayers." At the words: "Come to his help, ye saints of God. Come to meet him, ye angels of the Lord. Receive his soul and conduct it into the presence of the All Holy!" Dominic paid the debt we all must pay. It was noon, August 6, 1221. Procurator Rudolph washed the corpse, clothed it in the complete habit of the Order, and laid it upon the bier.

There the brethren kept constant vigil, alternating at praying the psalms. Externs also came and prayed near the holy remains, among them Prior Albert from St. Catherine's in Bologna. He experienced such transports of joy that he kissed the body, embraced it, and then exclaimed: "Blessed tidings! Master Dominic just told me that within a year I will be with him in Christ." Before the year had run its course, Prior Albert was dead. Rudolph also supervised the placing of the body in a wooden coffin, and nailed it shut with his own hands. He attested that no spices were enclosed in the coffin.

Cardinal Ugolino came from Venice to officiate at the obsequies on August 7 in the presence of many high church dignitaries, civil authorities, and the entire community. The coffin was then lowered into the vault and the tomb sealed with a stone slab, which was cemented into the masonry and flooring. No monument or inscription pointed out to churchgoers the silent resting place of this truly great man, buried in the position he himself had chosen, under the feet of his brethren.

GLORIFICATION

"Eternal rest give unto them, O Lord," the Church sings for the souls of her departed members, but this does not mean that the saints are sleeping. Dominic began working miracles and making mysterious visitations to earth as soon as he had left it. At the time of Dominic's death, Brother Giles, prior of the monastery in Brescia, had a vision in which he saw heaven opened. Two ladders, symbolic of contemplation and activity, were being lowered to earth. At the top of one stood Christ; upon the other, the Blessed Virgin. On a throne between the two ladders sat a preaching brother, his face covered with the capuche as is customary when burying the dead. Angels fluttered around the ladders, which were being drawn heavenward. As the gates of heaven closed, the apparition ended and Giles set out posthaste for Bologna, where he learned that Dominic had died at the very hour in which he had seen the vision. On the same day, as Brother Raoul was about to pray for Dominic's recovery at the memento for the living during Mass, he saw Dominic radiant in heavenly brightness and adorned with a golden crown, about to leave Bologna.

In spite of these signs of their Father's glorification in heaven, the brethren shut up shop as far as his canonization was concerned. The people of Bologna, however, were of a different opinion. There was no doubt in their minds that Dominic would send them help from heaven if they called upon him in their difficulties. When their prayers were answered, they came to the monastery and offered votive memorials in thanksgiving, asking that these testimonials be placed near the tomb. Others made gifts of money with the request that it be used to construct an enclosure around the grave, so that thoughtless visitors would not walk heedlessly over the sacred spot. The brethren remained strangely unyielding to these entreaties. They did not want to be accused of running a miracle factory. Even the miraculous cure of the youth Petronolus did not change their attitude. The boy had suffered for two years from a serious abdominal injury for which the physicians could give no help. The afflicted mother brought him to Dominic's grave, and he was cured on the spot. The miracle was reported to the brethren, but they letting it come in one ear and go out at the other, continued walking over their Father's grave without a twinge of conscience.

By 1233 popular devotion had become so intense that it was necessary to enlarge the church; consequently, the body had to be disinterred. While this building and expansion were in progress, the Founder's grave was unprotected from wind and rain. This shocking negligence opened the eyes of some of the brethren, and their justifiable criticism aroused the conscience of their companions. Indignation and repentance led to the resolve of transferring their Father's remains to the new church and there deposit them in a suitable tomb. Several brethren were sent to Rome to obtain the Pope's permission for the solemn transfer. Ugolino of Ostia, the friend of Dominic, who was now Pope Gregory IX, received them graciously, but called them to account for being so slow-gaited about their Father's canonization, whose holiness he doubted as little as that of the Apostles Peter and Paul. He granted the desired permission and sent the Archbishop of Ravenna to witness for him the opening of the relics. At St. Nicholas in Bologna the joy over this information was not unalloyed with fear as to the condition of the remains, because the grave had been neglected so long. The odor of mustiness and decay would not sharpen the devotion of the faithful.

In 1233 the General Chapter of the Order was scheduled to convene at Bologna, so the day preceding the first session was set for the translation. The brethren would have preferred to open the tomb secretly, but that was impossible. The Archbishop of Ravenna, the mayor of Bologna, and twelve city officials were present at the ceremony, which took place during the night between May 23 and 24, in the presence of these dignitaries, the capitular Fathers, and the members of St. Nicholas community. Under supervision of the procurator, the slab that overlaid the grave was raised and, to the relief of the brethren, a pleasant fragrance arose from the tomb, unlike any earthly perfume. When the coffin was opened, this delightful odor became so pronounced that no doubt was possible as to its source and significance. News of this unusual circumstance spread throughout Bologna like wildfire so that a large crowd was present the following morning to witness the solemn transfer. Jordan, the Master General of the Order, assisted by a number of senior brethren, carried the coffin from the old church into the new, which was soon filled with the same heavenly fragrance. Eight days later the coffin was again opened because many people had not been able to assist at the first celebration.

Jordan then took the head of the Saint in his hands, kissed it reverently, and offered it to those present to be likewise venerated. All again perceived the celestial perfume. It remained for days on their hands and clothing, and they were seized with the ardent desire that the Church would quickly ratify God's evident approval of Dominic's heroic holiness.

The flood of miracles which followed this translation prompted Pope Gregory IX to appoint a commission of enquiry into the life of Dominic and to begin at once the canonization process. This commission met at Bologna and Toulouse during the months of July and August, 1233, and took the depositions on oath from men and women who had lived with, or been well known to Dominic. Among these were Prior Ventura, who had been present at his last hours, Procurator Rudolph, William of Montferrat, Stephen of Spain, and Paul of Venice. There was also the evidence of those who remembered Dominic in his early missionary labors at Toulouse; perhaps the "younger women" whose conversation had pleased the tired preacher, and who had tried to provide better food and clothing for him. Then the reports of the numerous miracles had to be authenticated. By the close of the year the documents were sent to Rome to be closely re-examined. On July 13, 1234, Gregory IX solemnly canonized St. Dominic. The star which his godmother had seen on his brow at baptism was now lighting up the entire Church. We have the infallible pledge of Christ's Vicar that St. Dominic's well-balanced life of prayer and activity is worthy of our imitation, that he himself is close to God's throne and will offer the prayers of his clients to the Threefold Unity.

VIII
THE PERSONALITY

THE MAN

LOOKING back on the fifty-one years of St. Dominic's life, we are faced with the question of his personality, that which made him a distinct person, those individual characteristics which set him apart from his fellow men. Tradition has handed down to us so many traits concerning St. Dominic, that we may at least attempt his character study.

The salient point in St. Dominic's make-up is his highly endowed intellect. He is not to be classed among those emotional men, guided principally by their moods and feelings. In St. Dominic the intellect ruled; it held the reins and directed the course to be followed. During the years of philosophical and theological study at Gumiel and Palencia, Dominic developed his intellect to such an extent that thereafter he judged everything he saw or heard from an ethical viewpoint. Dominic remained a theologian all his life, not only because he always continued to study sacred doctrine, but also because in practical conduct he focused everything on God. There was an element of quiet reflection, the spirit of contemplation, in his character. He followed Diego's leading not merely out of respect for his Bishop, but also because Diego was on fire for every noble enterprise, no matter whether he

147

himself first thought of it, or if it was suggested to him by another. The idea of fighting the heretics with their own weapons came to Dominic during the night he spent in the house of the Albigensian innkeeper. While continuing their journey he discussed the plan with Bishop Diego, who later made it known to the legates at Montpellier. Dominic's peaceful missionary plan was so clear and logical that many think he must have had models to build on. But in spite of all the discussion he had with Diego, the similarity between his plan and that of St. Francis, and the unfavorable pattern of the Waldensians and Albigensians. St. Dominic merits the honor of first conceiving the plan of converting heretics by teaching the gospel truths in absolute poverty and leaving it as a sacred heritage to his Order.

The same holds true of the composition, altering, and final draft of the Constitutions of his Order. This is a masterpiece of clear thinking, precise expression, and logical co-ordination of component elements, in which every word points unmistakably to the final goal, the salvation of souls through preaching the Word of God. The Dominican way of life is like a mighty river, carrying the water of its tributaries to the ocean, the quiet waters of contemplation united with the torrent of activity in the service of mankind. Dominic blended the stern monastic discipline of the monks and canons with the free play necessary in an Order whose members, old and young, were sent throughout the world to preach the Gospel. In establishing the Order and dispersing the first brethren, Dominic often had to suit his actions to circumstances, at one time waiting patiently, then again urgently pressing forward, apparently hastening the accomplishment of the project. Yet each procedure was the only correct conduct in that particular case. His answer to the cautions of the brethren and his friends sounded strange to them: "I know what I am about." He knew without fail what he was doing, because he did everything under the guidance of his sharp intellect.

Does this make Dominic a cold intellectual devoid of the heart's warmth and understanding? If by the heart is meant the boiling over of the emotions, easily influenced by quickly succeeding impressions, then it is quite true, Dominic had no place for this sort of thing, either with himself or with his followers. He did not even allow it among the nuns; that is why the letter written by him to the Sisters at Madrid is so steady-nerved. But if by the heart we mean the deep, powerful inclination of the will toward a high ideal, which carries along with it the operations of the sensitive appetite and even lays hold of the physical heart, then Dominic was not cold-hearted. The sacrifices which he made for the attainment of his ideal and the way he kept to his course when ill winds were blowing, are positive proofs that his heart was richly blessed with noble emotions.

The only serious soul struggle which Dominic had to endure arose from the opposition between the two ideals animating him. As newly ordained priest he had joined the cathedral chapter at Osma, shaping his life according to the Rule of St. Augustine with all the fervor that belongs to young manhood. During the years of the Albigensian missionary labors, the curtain rose on a new picture, that of an Apostle preaching the Gospel to all mankind in perfect poverty. This ideal was higher than the first, and his intellect told him that he could rightfully sacrifice a lesser good in favor of a greater; but the thought of being disloyal to his first choice blew up a gale within him. His clear judgment subdued this emotional conflict; for the sake of the higher ideal he was willing to have the stone of fickleness laid at his door. But the amount of interior torture this step cost him can only be appreciated by one who has been ground in the same mill. The depths of this grief corresponded to the exultant joy he later experienced when the Pope requested him to shape the Constitutions of his new Order on the framework of an already approved Rule. He could now remain true to his first ideal while affirming it in a higher form.

Dominic's procedure in the matter of absolute poverty proves that he was not stubbornly wedded to his own opinion. He did not incorporate absolute poverty in the first draft of the Constitutions lest an imprudent measure endanger the approbation of the Order. During the interval before the first General Chapter, he tolerated revenues and traveling money. It was only after the majority had voted in favor of absolute poverty that he insisted on its rigid observance.

A keen, penetrating intellect and a firm, self-sacrificing will intent on a high ideal were the natural good dispositions which God used as a foundation for the work which, through Dominic, would reap such a world-wide vintage of souls.

THE ASCETIC

Baptism transforms the child of Adam into a child of God, but does not remove the consequences of Adam's sin; it directs man's course heavenward, but does not cut him off from earthly moorings. The interior discord stirred up by original sin weakens Christ's image in the human soul and makes the way to heaven a hard road to travel. In the language of spiritual writers, a conversion is necessary: getting rid of the bad blood of earthly desires, subduing our sensual instincts, and then modeling our spiritual life after the example of Christ. That is the sum and substance of Christian asceticism. The Albigensians, believing that everything material, including the human body, is essentially evil, created by the devil, were led to an exaggerated self-immolation. Dominic knew that man had been created by God as a well-ordered clockwork, but sin had thrown the stone of confusion in this divine masterwork, the harmony of which can only be restored by mortification and penance. We find traces of this holy austerity already in Dominic as a boy. His mother had told him that the Child Jesus had not been laid in a soft bed, but in a rough manger. The following morning she found her son asleep on the floor. That was asceticism practiced from its highest motive, the desire to resemble Christ. We have seen how, as a student, Dominic denied himself the use of wine. Later, during his apostolic journeys, he quenched his thirst at the village well before entering the rectory or monastery so that dry lips would not lead him to excessive wine drinking. He was also moderate in the use of food. As Superior he always insisted that the brethren be served two separate dishes, but he himself only ate of the first and then sat and listened to the table reading. Sometimes, it is true, he fell asleep at table, fatigued from his preaching, journeys, and vigils. He scourged himself to the blood three times every night, in expiation for his own sins, to obtain forgiveness for the sins of all mankind, and for the relief of the souls in purgatory. Although these practices are praiseworthy, Dominic's forgetfulness of self and thoughtfulness of others are better suited for our imitation than his hair shirts and scourgings. He founded thirty monasteries and saw to it that every brother had a cell, but he himself died in Brother Moneta's cell because he had none of his own.

Bodily austerity is necessary, although not in the same manner or degree for everybody. But far more important is spiritual discipline, holding our mind and will in bondage. Tradition assures us that Dominic exercised an arduous asceticism of the spirit. He renounced all unnecessary conversation and concentrated his thoughts on God and the salvation of souls. We are told that he spoke only of God and divine things; in other words, he considered all things in relation to God and judged their importance in proportion as they promoted God's honor and the salvation of souls. That implies a rigid asceticism of the spirit, retrenching all distractions and aiming directly at the "one thing necessary."

Dominic disciplined his will by bending it to the wishes of his superiors. Diego had good reasons for choosing his Subprior as traveling companion; he accommodated himself so perfectly to his Bishop's plans that it seemed he had no personal opinions. The future would show that he certainly had his own ideas, but he knew that well-timed silence is more eloquent than speech. His conduct toward Bishop Faulkes was the same, and later, at the time of the General Chapter, he submitted himself entirely to the directions of the definitors by parting with his pet scheme of converting the Cuman Tartars. More than one brother deposed at the canonization process that Dominic never corrected an erring brother at the time of the offense, but waited until the guilty individual had regained his composure, and he himself was prepared to insist on the perfect observance of the Rule and Constitutions with both gentleness and firmness.

Dominic's serenity in the midst of constant vexations was not the polished composure of worldlings, but the outward indication of interior peace, the splendor radiating from a quiet soul, the result of self-effacement in divine love, and the wordless expression of his reverence for his fellow men. Not to become presumptuous in prosperity, not to despond in adversity, but always to remain steady-nerved in spite of unjust demands, burdensome proposals, daily drudgery, and occasional turmoils requires heroic self-possession. This interior and exterior calmness, the coinage of a superior asceticism, gave Dominic an almost irresistible influence over others, and enabled him to attract, to recall, and to guide them in the desired direction. A quotation from Constantine of Orvieto will prove this point: "The Venerable Father, the Servant of God, Dominic, was a man of distinguished manners. His tranquillity could only be disturbed by compassion for the afflictions of others. A mere glance from his eyes drew hearts to him without difficulty. In his dealings with souls he seldom failed to accomplish his first designs in their regard. In the daytime he was affable to all who came to him; during the night no one surpassed him in prayer and vigils. He was genial toward all who came to him because he loved them all and was beloved by them in return. It had become second nature for him to rejoice with the joyful and weep with the sorrowful."

THE MYSTIC

Dominic did not conceal his desire of attracting the brilliant University students to his Order, but lie also made it clear that he was not organizing a Savant Society where his followers could live the life of a clam between sermons and lectures. The Founder of the Preaching Brethren was a man of prayer. All his early biographers make prayer the mainspring of his life. Witness after witness at the canonization process spoke of this characteristic. Paul of Venice noted that often on his apostolic journeys Dominic would say to his companion, "Go on ahead and let us think of our Saviour," or he would intone the "Ave Maris Stella" or "Veni Creator Spiritus." But it was especially during the quiet night hours, when he thought himself alone in the Church, that the brethren overheard him praying vocally and with gestures, pausing in silence now and then as if he were listening to another. "I have never seen a man to whom prayer was more habitual," was the testimony of the Abbot of St. Paul.

It is not likely that God would withhold mystical graces from a man who strained every nerve seeking the divine intimacy. These graces are the ordinary consequence of holding on through thick and thin in the spiritual life, and it is to enable all to reach this state that God fits out every soul with the Gifts of the Holy Ghost at Baptism. All souls may — indeed, should — reach the state wherein the Holy Ghost enlightens them on the highest truths of faith through the Gifts of Wisdom and Understanding, and takes them by the hand to teach them how to use earthly things from heavenly motives by the Gifts of Knowledge and Counsel. The three remaining Gifts, Piety, Fear, and Fortitude, electrify the will and help it leap over barriers in the accomplishment of the good recognized by the intellect and loved by the will; they impel to heroic deeds which appear without rhyme or reason to ordinary Christians. Dominic's fervor in prayer and his spiritual transports point unmistakably to the intervention of the Holy Ghost and satisfy the requirements of this traditional interpretation of mysticism.

If we give the term mysticism a more restricted meaning and define it as the possession of charisms, those extraordinary gifts of grace intended primarily for the healing or instruction of others, then Dominic is also a true mystic because his life abounds in these eminent gifts, "pressed down, shaken together, and running over." He was often favored with true visions and ecstasies, not phantasies resulting from an overwrought imagination. The two young men who entered the refectory, placed bread before the brethren and then disappeared as mysteriously as they had come, and the young man who accompanied Dominic from San Sisto to Santa Sabina, are examples of such images beheld by the physical eyes not only of the Saint, but also of his companions. When Saints Peter and Paul appeared to Dominic while he was praying in the Basilica at Rome and gave a book and staff to him, he did not have these objects in his hands when the vision ended. It had been a sensible or corporal vision. He once told the brethren that the Order would soon lose four members, two by death and two by backsliding. He had not foreseen this with his bodily eyes, but in an intellectual vision. The prediction was soon fulfilled. Jordan of Saxony maintains that the dispersion of the brethren was the result of a prophetic illumination.

Dominic was not given to talking about his spiritual state. If a few words on the subject did accidentally escape him, he quickly regretted it, as if it were a grievous slip of the tongue. This was the case when, to praise the divine goodness, he confided to the Prior of Casamare that God had never refused a petition he had earnestly prayed for, and again when on his deathbed he spoke of the immaculately preserved lily of chastity; so it is very probable that his contemporaries did not know half of what took place in his soul.

The miracle in which a saint serves as God's instrument in the performance of an action which surpasses the limits of nature, such as restoring life to a dead body, is the effect of a grace Gratis Datae. In the canonization process we find two instances where Dominic raised the dead to life at San Sisto in Rome. One concerns the young Napoleon; the other is related as follows. "One of the workmen at San Sisto was crushed to death under some falling masonry. The brethren were afraid that the people would positively turn against them because strange tales were already being spread concerning this new-fledged Order. Dominic noticed that his disciples were frightened almost out of their wits, so he had the dead body brought to him and by the power of his prayer restored the man to life."

Close intimacy with God is followed by the

devil's bad blood as unerringly as the needle points to the pole. This bad blood is not missing in Dominic's life. Blessed Cecilia relates that Dominic would often gather the Sisters in the garden attached to the Convent of San Sisto, and sitting with them there by the side of a little stream which ran through the grounds, would discourse on the things of God. On one such occasion the Sisters were alarmed by the sudden appearance among them of a strange and hideous reptile, and some of them, womanlike, were running away in terror when Dominic, recognizing Satan's favorite trick in this attempt to disturb the conference, made the Sign of the Cross and commanded the monster to depart; whereupon it plunged into the stream and disappeared. Then there is Constantine of Orvieto's account of the recluse Benedicta who lived in a cell adjoining St. Nicholas Church at Bologna. She had become possessed by the devil. After Dominic freed her from him, she fell into a frivolous and wanton life; so he sometimes permitted the devil to vent his spleen against her, because an occasional thorn in the flesh kept her on the narrow path.

God sometimes gives such extraordinary powers as the ability to perform exorcisms and miracles, to prophesy, and see visions to men whose moral life is not blameless. The crucial test of Catholic mysticism is whether the individual practices virtue to a heroic degree under the influence of the Gifts of the Holy Ghost. Dominic was a mystic of this class, strong in faith, his heart devoted to God alone and all his faculties employed in the service of his fellow men for love of God. If we understand a mystic to be a person who watches over a guarded flame and who does not advance to share with others the enjoyment of his fire, a hermit who avoids human intercourse, or a monk who hides in his cell, then Dominic was not a mystic because he left solitude and went to men. He first fixed his eyes on God and then preached to all men what the Divine Fire had seared into his soul, thereby becoming not less a contemplative but communicating to others the overflow of contemplation.

THE APOSTLE

God called Dominic to apostolic labors through circumstances which left no doubt that the invitation was a true one. In order to make the gospel truths leap to the eye and strengthen the hands of his hearers, it is sufficient that the apostle meditates in the manner of an ascetic, considering the practical application of Christ's words in his own spiritual life and in that of those to whom he will preach. But his words will bear more fruit if this meditation has been replaced by contemplation, if the truths of faith have been lovingly considered under the influence of the gifts of the Holy Ghost, their importance clarified in the cloudless rays of divine light and their lessons applied to the preacher's personal life in an intimate and heroic manner. The maxim, "physician, heal thyself" is never more true than in a spiritual application. Nothing so upsets the laity as to see the preacher's private life giving the lie to the great truths he expounds from the pulpit. People readily make the resolution of doing at least what is necessary for salvation if they know that the preacher himself is doing it a hundred times more.

Many depositions at the canonization process refer to Dominic as a preacher and apostle. Brother Ventura stated that "he spoke only to God and of God." To speak to God in contemplation is the apostle's preparation for preaching, for how could he speak of God if he is not already on speaking terms with God? This rule did not make Dominic a skeleton at the feast. Jordan of Saxony says that "none was ever more joyous than he, and none a better companion." Brother Amizo called Dominic a torrential preacher and an enthusiast for souls. Brother John the Spaniard spoke of him as "bringing the heretics to bay by preaching and disputation, and regaining many wanderers to the fold of Holy Mother Church." Brother Rudolph testified that Dominic's zeal in preaching and hearing confessions often moved both himself and his hearers to tears. The Cistercian Abbot William of St. Paul's in Narbonne gave Dominic the distinction of excelling all his contemporaries in zeal for souls, being so unflagging in preaching that "day and night, in houses, in the fields, on the roads, he never ceased to proclaim the Word of God, enjoining on his brethren to do the same and to let their conversation be of God alone."

These testimonies make it clear that Dominic was a trenchant apostle, sniping at the heretics with the spiritual weapons of preaching and disputation in season and out of season. His motive in this war to the death was not hatred. Blessed Jordan makes use of a choice expression, saying that "Dominic took all into the arms of his love, wide as the church-door."

The situation in Spain was also fuel for Dominic's apostolic fire. The Spanish rulers had attacked the Moors by force of arms; but if military power was to determine the issue, then how would these enemies of Christianity ever be converted to the faith? Diego had planned a peaceful missionary project among them. The danger of imprisonment or martyrdom at the hands of the fanatical Moors did not frighten him or his Subprior. In later years Dominic earnestly desired to work at the conversion of the Cuman Tartars, but the General Chapter pulled the check string of this project. Two incentives urged him to the heathen missions: the crown of martyrdom awaiting the missionary and the fact that this type of preaching is the highest expression of the purpose for which he had founded his Order.

Dominic's idea of the apostolate was unlimited both as to place and method. He stepped out of the little groove of his individual life and put into practice Christ's words, "Preach the Gospel to every creature." His impassioned cry to God may be stated as, "Let me give Thee all the souls of all the world." Contemplation and mystical life were not to be considered as walls separating the mystic from the tumult of existence, but as doors uniting the two rooms of prayer and activity. Dominic accomplished in himself this broad notion of preaching Christ to all and left it as the ideal to be aimed at by future generations of Dominicans. As a philosopher he knew that man can only love what he knows. That is why the Saviour in the various phases of His mortal life was the central theme of his preaching; Christ in the three years' public ministry, speaking to the multitude in the sermon on the mount, addressing the people on the shore from the pulpit of Peter's boat, instructing Nicodemus, threatening the Pharisees with dreadful woes, and convicting the Sadducees of heresy. The stricture, "Your actions shout so lustily that we cannot hear your preaching," could not be thrown at Dominic, because Blessed Jordan tells us that he imitated the Divine Model so perfectly that for his spiritual sons it did not make a great deal of difference whether they thought of and looked at their Father or Christ in order to be reanimated with the ideal of preaching the Gospel to all men.

THE SAINT

The task of becoming a saint is a twofold process; St. Paul describes it as putting off the old man and putting on the new. The putting-off the old is the casting aside of sins and vices; the taking-on the new is the acquisition of heroic virtues. Since all virtues which really deserve that name are founded on and controlled by charity, it is true to say that sinlessness and charity are sanctity. Because charity excludes mortal sin and in its development brings about a decrease of deliberate venial sin, it follows that perfect charity and sanctity are cast in the same mold. God's command to the chosen people in the Old Testament, "Be ye holy, because I your God am holy" (Lev. 11:44), binds all men to aim at this type of sanctity, which may be hidden so that even the possessor thereof is unaware of it and his acquaintances notice only vaguely the grandeur concealed under that quiet exterior, but before which they would fall to their knees if they fully realized its presence. After what we have said of Dominic as an ascetic, mystic, and apostle, there can be no doubt that he was a saint such as we must all strive to become. If anyone considers it an easy thing to preserve one's virginity for half a century and to spurn everything earthly for love of God and souls, then let him try it.

Sanctity may also be considered under a more limited aspect, as the second-to-none perfection of those privileged individuals in whom God deigns to reveal Himself as Sanctity and Sanctifier. Saints of this description are like towering mountain peaks, encouraging their fellow men on the plain below to do at least what is necessary for salvation. Their interior holiness manifests itself outwardly; for the sun of perfect charity must break through the clouds, sometimes in one sublime, heroic act, like martyrdom. A martyr sacrifices his life utterly for the faith or to preserve intact a Christian virtue, and thus gives to God all he can give, in supreme proof of his love for Him. It may even be that before this occurrence the individual was not a model of virtue, but by thus going through fire and water for love of God all his sins are expiated in the blood of Christ. The soul has put off the rags of sin and donned the mantle of perfect charity. This transformation obtains the martyr's immediate entrance into the beatific vision. Dominic did not procure the red trophy, even though he ardently longed for martyrdom of the most severe kind.

Perfect charity has other ways of coming to light than by that of actual martyrdom. The faith of such a soul furnishes it with a wholly supernatural system of values, giving it a deep insight into the final purpose of life's apparently insignificant details, and impelling charity to deeds which appear extravagant to the ordinary Christian. It was this profound faith which inspired Dominic's idea of absolute poverty and gave him no rest until he had succeeded in making its practice a necessary part of his Order. This ideal seemed overdone to many of his contemporaries. During Dominic's lifetime it was an attainable standard, but in later centuries altered circumstances have made it necessary to moderate its exact execution.

The saint must give such exterior expression of his interior devotion as will excite others to practice piety, to cast aside lukewarmness, and rise above mere external exactitude. Brother John of Bologna asserted that, "When serving his Mass I often saw tears trickling down his cheeks as he turned to take the ablution after Holy Communion. He gazed upon the Sacred Host with such rapt attention that it seemed as if he beheld the Saviour with his bodily eyes." He is described to us as leaving his choir stall during the Divine Office and passing up and down among the brethren, exhorting them, "More bravely, my brothers!" His first care when arriving at a town on his missionary treks was to seek out the church, there to greet his Sacramental Lord and spend all his free time in Christ's presence. "Burning the candle at both ends," many may have thought. At one time he received hospitality in the Cathedral Chapter at Castres; when dinner time came the monks wondered where he could be. It was then that Prior Matthew saw him in ecstasy, levitated several feet above the floor before the altar.

Another necessity for a person who has been set up by God as an example of holiness for his fellow men is that he pass through the night of the senses and of the spirit, that he experience disquietude and fear for his own perseverance. Did Dominic pass through these experiences? Let us recall how he ordinarily spent the night hours, after a day of preaching and laboring for souls. He kneels alone in the dark church. He prays, at first quietly, then louder; he wrings his hands, he moans, he cries aloud. What grief is tormenting him? It is the mystery of redemption. Jesus brought the glad tidings. Dominic had just passed another day preaching the gospel truths. But who believes these truths? Why is the number of believers so small? Jesus proved His love for mankind; He loved us to the end, the death on the cross. Where is our reciprocal love? What will be the eternal fate of unbelieving, unloving mankind? This darkness concerning human destiny is Dominic's night. He does not fear only for himself but for all men, for the just and for sinners. He grabs his discipline and scourges himself to blood in order to fill up in his body the sufferings of Christ for wayward mankind. Dominic was not only an image of the Saviour preaching the glad tidings, but also a continuation of the suffering Redeemer, sacrificing Himself for our redemption.

The principal feast of St. Dominic is observed throughout the Roman Catholic Church on August 4, but the proper Office of the feast is confined to the Dominican Order and the Order of Friars Minor, just as Dominicans celebrate the proper Office of St. Francis of Assisi on October 4. The festival Office of St. Dominic starts in with an invitation to rejoice, addressed to Spain as his birthplace, to Bologna as the city of his farewell to this earthly exile, and then to the entire Catholic Church which he illuminated as a morning star in the midst of a cloud. Two other feasts have been granted by the Church to the Dominican Order in honor of its Founder. On May 24 is commemorated the translation of the Saint's relics, which occurred during the generalship of Blessed Jordan. The scriptural lessons for this feast compare him to the prophet Elias. The miraculous phenomenon of the statue of St. Dominic in Suriano, which transformed that hitherto unknown town into a place of pilgrimage in honor of the Saint during the nineteenth century, is recalled on September 25.

Perhaps because of the false charge of being the author of the Inquisition, Dominic remained for many years an unknown, or at least unnoticed, Saint. But the modern revival of the Rosary devotion, with which St. Dominic is inseparably united as founder, did much to stir up his popularity among the faithful. According to a tradition mentioned in many papal encyclicals, it was during Dominic's missionary years in France that our Blessed Lady revealed to him a project forged from all eternity in God's mind. Dominic, we are told, realized that although his nuns at Prouille were converting many heretics by their example and prayers, his own preaching was practically abortive. As an apostle he was pouring water into a sieve. We must remember that the Albigensians denied such essential Christian mysteries as Creation, the Incarnation, Redemption, Descent of the Holy Ghost, the Ascension, and the Assumption. While in the town of Albi, a stronghold of heresy, Dominic asked the Virgin Mother to teach him how to refute such falsehoods, and in answer she inspired him with a new method of preaching. "Wonder not that until now thou hast gathered so little fruit from thy labors. Thou hast spent them on barren soil, not yet watered with the dew of divine grace. When God willed to renew the face of the earth He began by sending down the fertilizing rain of the Angelic Salutation. Therefore, preach my Psalter, and thou wilt obtain an abundant harvest."

This assignment Dominic accomplished so well that many Popes have not hesitated to call him the founder of the Rosary devotion, just as St. Bernard is called the founder of the Cistercian Order, although his actual work was its propagation far and wide. Pope Leo XIII's repeated encyclicals on the Rosary quickened the devotion of the laity to St. Dominic, through whom Mary gave the Rosary to mankind. This assertion has been passed in review by many historians. Some say that the Rosary antedates Dominic, others that it came after him. It is true that long before his time Our Fathers and Hail Marys were checked and numbered by a string of beads, but it is only since the thirteenth century that we find the division into decades or groups of ten, separated by larger beads called Our Fathers, and meditation on a particular scene of the life of Christ or Mary during each decade. There is also the strong family resemblance between the Rosary devotion and the Dominican Order; both are a combination of two apparently contradictory elements. The ideal Dominic set before his Preaching Brethren and Sisters is the harmonious blending of contemplation and activity; the Rosary offers to all the faithful a means of fusing mental and vocal prayer.

What is the twentieth-century implication

of the star on Dominic's forehead? The answer is found in the Mass for his feast — "guiding men on virtue's way" by the preaching of sacred truth in opposition to false ideologies, by mortification and self-denial instead of catering to the senses, by prayerful activity in place of much distracted bustle and turmoil.

"Long the wheat-grain lay in hiding
Beyond the cloud the star residing;
As the Morning Star
But God's hand that all doth sway,
Joseph's bones commands to blossom,
And the star of morn to brighten, Guiding men
on virtue's way."

- *Sequence from the Mass of St. Dominic*